THE FACES OF STRUGGLES

SUCH AS CANCERS

ARE ON THE JOURNEY TO GOD'S GLORY!

By: Alfancena Millicent Barrett

JAZZY KITTY PUBLISHING

The Faces of Struggles Such as Cancers

Are On The Journey to God's Glory!

By: Alfancena Millicent Barrett

Cover design by: Anelda L. Ballard

Cover Photograph by: Alfancena Millicent Barrett

Logo designs by: Andre M. Saunders/Leroy Grayson

Editor: Ingrid Price and Peggy Smoot

Assistant Editor: Anelda L. Ballard

Photographs by: Alfancena Millicent Barrett

© 2010 Alfancena Barrett 1-334726081

ISBN 978-0-9843255-7-3

ISBN 0-9843255-7-3

Library of Congress Control Number: 2010930127

For Worldwide Distribution. Printed in the United States of America
Published by Jazzy Kitty Greetings Marketing & Publishing, LLC dba Jazzy Kitty Publishing. Utilizing Microsoft Publishing Software.

ACKNOWLEDGMENTS

First, I would like to thank God for choosing me as a vessel to bring GLORY to His name. Thanks to all of my family members and friends who served as my source of strength and encouragement.

Special thanks to my brother Cleve who spent part of his summer vacation proofreading parts of my story.

Thanks to my brother Lambert who, when he read about how he helped in my maturity, had questions, but was okay with what I had written.

Thanks to my pastor and my entire Shiloh family in Wilmington, Delaware who has been there for me through it all. Thanks to all those who were excited that I was sharing my testimony in written form.

Thanks to my co-workers, parents, and students of the Child Development Center and Delaware Technical and Community College for being there for me throughout my struggles.

Thanks to my neighbors who were there to help me when I needed help. Thanks to all of my relatives and friends who have submitted their thoughts describing how I have witnessed to them through my trials.

Thanks to Sister Ruth Bright and Brother James for the information they provided in connection with getting my book published.

Thanks to my new found sister Anelda, my publisher who I believe was God's answer to my prayer.

DEDICATIONS

This book is dedicated to the loving memories of family and friends, who were diagnosed after me, with the exception of Mary, left me to carry on the fight. I met Mary shortly before she volunteered to be my chauffeur to my doctors' appointments, even though the doctor told her she was living on borrowed time.

Roslyn Barrett - mom
Victor Barrett - dad
Villair Barrett - brother
Sytre Barrett - sister-in-law
Yvonne Byfield - aunt
Veronica Byfield - aunt
Harry Mignott - friend
Veronica Higgins -Friend
Lorna Reid - Friend
Gale Douglas - Friend
Mary Jernigan - Friend

My promise to all of you is that I will continue this fight down here until Jesus needs my help up there.

Helen White, my sister in Christ who now struggles with the return of breast cancer after 18 years; fight on my sister because with God healing is possible.

Yvonne Brown, my adopted niece who survived both colon and uterus cancer at a young age. After that ordeal God has blessed her with a husband and two beautiful daughters. May God continue to bless her to be strong, free of cancer and to be an anchor to her family.

TABLE OF CONTENTS

TABLE OF CONTENTS

TABLE OF CONTENTS

INTRODUCTION

This book is my testimony of how God used me through life's struggles to bring Glory to His name. It tells of how He prepared me with the help of my family, from the time of my birth to the present, using an imperfect body and person to carry out His will. A testimony of how my walk with God has helped me to understand how insignificant the physical body is and the power of the Spirit of God from within. When the Spirit lives within, it shines outwardly for others to see.

Friends and relatives submitted contributions, of how I have inspired them on this journey. I was taken aback when so many people with whom I have been in contact told me I have been an inspiration to them. My prayer since then has been that God would keep me humble so that His will would be done because it was not about me, it is all about Him.

My story tells of the powerful message that God is true to His promises, and how He uses people to carry out those promises. I have come to witness that God, through Jesus Christ, is the head of the healing process, followed by doctors, medication and the people with whom He surrounded me.

It is indicated in I Peter 1:7 (KJV) " *That the trials of your faith, being much more precious than of gold that perisheth, though it be tried with fire, might be found unto praise and honour and glory at the appearing of Jesus Christ.*"

i

THE FACES OF STRUGGLES SUCH AS CANCERS

ARE ON THE JOURNEY TO GOD'S GLORY!

Alfancena Millicent Barrett

CHAPTER 1

HOW GOD PREPARED ME

My Entrance into This World

I was born to Roslyn and Victor Barrett on December 9th, 1960. This happened in the district of Benbow, the parish of Saint Catherine and the country of Jamaica. My parents were living in another district called Riversdale, but my mom always went home to my grandmother's house to have her children. She told me that she was expecting me a week later than the day of my birth. She had all my clothes washed, and was getting ready to iron them when she got the warning that I was ready to come. They had to travel a long distant to Benbow. It's moments like these that I find myself really missing my mom because I would have loved to have asked her the reason for traveling to my grandmother's home to have her babies, and how she endured those long trips

On the day of my birth, I learnt from my aunt that it was a happy and sad one. I was born with a congenital defect of my right leg. My aunt told me after the death of my mother that my mom cried when she saw my leg. My mom never shared that with me. My mom did share with me that she took me to the doctor sometime after my birth. She said the doctor told her to bring me back when I started to walk. She did not say how soon after my birth, but the way my aunt related the story it must have been soon

THE FACES OF STRUGGLES SUCH AS CANCERS ARE ON THE JOURNEY TO GOD'S GLORY!

Alfancena Millicent Barrett

after.

My mom oftentimes tried to describe what my leg looked like before it was corrected. My parents only had one baby picture of my elder brother; there was no evidence to show the extent of the defect. I guess it was because he was their first born, and cameras were not as popular as they are today. Because of that, I had to use my imagination when she described the condition of my leg to me. She said my lower right leg was bent outward. My mom said when I started to walk, I walked leaning to my right side.

When I was in high school on the netball team (a game similar to basketball) I went with my school to another district to challenge another team. While there, I saw a girl walking the way my mother described my manner of walking prior to corrective action being taken. I said to myself then, my mother was a smart woman. If my mother had not taken immediate action to correct my leg defect, I would not have been walking upright, as I do today.

After my father's funeral, as I was going through all of the papers at my parents' house I discovered something interesting. I was the only one of the five children who was dedicated a month after birth. My dedication certificate was different from my brothers' and sister's. It was the only one with a picture of Jesus blessing the little children. This made me wonder why that was so. My mother must have prayed a prayer like Hannah's because at the age of eleven, I was the first of their children to accept

Jesus as my personal Savior. Again, I wish my mom was here to provide answers to some of my most pressing questions, and help me to really learn more about who I am.

My mom gave me an explanation for what she thought happened to my leg. One day during her pregnancy, as she was cleaning, she bent down to sweep under the bed and, when she got up, she felt pain and sickness. She wondered if she could have broken my leg then. I have thought about this from time to time, and attribute my strong dislike for things stored under my bed to this. I prefer the area underneath my bed to be clean and free from clutter. Although I do not remember this, I was told that I spent my toddler years in the hospital and rehabilitation facility.

Memories of My Early Years

I remembered being on the bus a lot with my mom going back and forth for doctor visits. My memory served me well as I recall being on the "country" bus as so it was called because it travelled from the rural area to the city. I recall trips on the city bus, the Jamaica Omnibus Service or J.O.S bus as it was called, which was the public bus system in the city of Kingston, Jamaica. I loved the movement of the trees and cane fields while driving on the "country" bus. I loved seeing the river flowing as we passed by, and would sometimes fall asleep before getting to the flat-bridge, one of the landmark bridges in Jamaica, and had to be awoken by my mom. On the city bus, I had memories of passing a lot of people, and

THE FACES OF STRUGGLES SUCH AS CANCERS ARE ON THE JOURNEY TO GOD'S GLORY!

Alfancena Millicent Barrett

was fascinated by all the buildings. I remember having so much fun during trips to see the doctor when my mom, would buy popcorn which contained a prize ring inside. I got a kick out of coming home to "show off" my ring to my brothers. My mom liked dressing me in bangles on those trips, which made me felt very pretty.

I remembered going to Middlesex Basic School (preschool) for a little while, I can still recall the smell and the taste of the fried dumplings with butter that was served for lunch. On the way to school in the mornings spray planes would fly overhead spraying pesticides on the nearby banana plantations which felt a little creepy. When I was home and heard the spray planes flying overhead, I would rush outside to see them. I did not express my feelings to anyone because, as long as I was with my brothers, I felt safe. I left that school at some point in time to return to the rehabilitation center.

On my return home from the rehabilitation center, I remember going to Ms. Idel Basic School, which was close to home. On the first day at that school I experienced an embarrassment. I pooped on myself and had to be sent by the teacher, to an outhouse toilet. I had no recollection of who helped to clean me up. One of the jewels from that school was the friendship bond that I formed with the teacher's granddaughter, which is still very strong today. She is one of the persons I can call on whenever I am in need of assistance.

I remember wearing a special orthopedic shoe with iron braces on the

Alfancena Millicent Barrett

sides which extended up above my knee. That device called caliper which was equipped with knee padding aided in the reconstruction of my right leg. When I outgrew the shoe mom took me back to the doctor's office to get a replacement; however, we were disappointed to find that size that I needed was not available. Upon expressing our disappointment to the doctor, he advised that since I was progressing so well, that I could forego the orthopedic shoe replacement. I was a very active child, from what I can remember, and from the stories which have been told to me.

One morning when I woke up, my knee cap was out of place; it was on the outer side of my right leg. We then realized that my leg was not fully healed, and another trip to Mona Rehabilitation would be required.

That was the place where I remembered starting my elementary education. Upon arrival at "Mona Rehab", as it so fondly called. I found out that at five plus years of age I was too old for the toddler department, which was where I would have preferred to have been assigned. I was stripped of the clothes I wore from home and was issued the center's clothes. The only article of clothing that I did not remove was my underwear because they did not have any. The laundry for the day had not come in yet. The caregiver promised my mom that she would wash my underwear and secure them safely until she returned; however, it was never returned. I asked almost every day, but eventually I stopped asking. The lost of that underwear was disappointing because I really loved it.

My dad brought the underwear from the United States on his last farm work trip. It was pretty white underwear with lace in the back. The memory of that special underwear is etched in my mind, and even to this day, whenever I see a little girl with lace underwear on I experience a flashback. The laundry came later that day after my mom was gone. I was allowed to take clothes from the trolley to put in my drawers. I can't remember how many pieces of clothing we were allowed to take, but I remember taking the prettiest outfits. I have no recollection of what the center underwear looked like.

While at "Mona Rehab," I wished I had a wheel chair or crutches like the other children. They looked real cool; however, I learned later that they were not as mobile as I was.

The day of my scheduled surgery arrived. We got in an ambulance which took us from "Mona Rehab" to the hospital. I remembered the nurse talking to me while I was lying on the stretcher. I was given anesthesia which made my eye lids heavy and a little while later, I was out. I woke up in the recovery room screaming, because when I tried to get up I could not. I was encased in plaster of Paris from the area above my waist down to the toes of my right foot. A nurse came over and comforted me. The long and short of it was that procedure was necessary in order to correct my knee cap. I can't say how long I wore that cast, but I remember the cast, eventually being changed to one that went from my thigh down to my toes. At some point in time, the cast removed and I was ready to attend school on campus.

THE FACES OF STRUGGLES SUCH AS CANCERS
ARE ON THE JOURNEY TO GOD'S GLORY!

Alfancena Millicent Barrett

As early as I can remember, I was always loved by almost everyone who crossed my path. One day while waiting in the courtyard of the hospital on one of my visits the people sitting with us were very friendly towards me and found me to be very fascinating. My mom turned to me and said "You sure do make a lot of friends just like Jesus. Maybe this likeness is because you were born in the month that we celebrate Jesus' birth." I felt very special then and I still do today when I remember her remarks about my Jesus-like personality.

Before I started going to school at "Mona Rehab" center I was used to receiving a mid morning snack. The snack would consist of a cup of Milo (a chocolate-type drink that was served warm or cold), and fruit or fruit juice. That would not be a part of my morning routine once I started school, but because of my special connection with people, it continued longer than it should have. The caregivers would leave my snack everyday on my nightstand and when I got a break, I would get it. One day I came back late from getting my snack and had to get on the elevator by myself to go up to the classroom. I could not say for sure what happened, but I remembered the elevator was dark, which was frightening to me. Another thing that frightened me at that school was quarry dump trucks. Near the rehab center was a quarry which was adjacent to a road that was busy with dump trucks passing by. The school was not exactly near the road, but I could see the trucks passing, which frightened me. I just thought they looked ugly, and I refused to go out in the school yard by myself when

THE FACES OF STRUGGLES SUCH AS CANCERS
ARE ON THE JOURNEY TO GOD'S GLORY!

Alfancena Millicent Barrett

they were passing. One pleasant memory for sure at that school was learning the song, "Have You Ever Seen a Lassie."

I am not a swimmer, but I spent quite some time in the pool for therapy. Some of my friends learned to swim, but I did not. I would hold on to the rails of the pool and walk around it, even in the deep section. I was a very active child, in spite of my disability at the time, and the adults around me at times were puzzled. We were free to explore the grounds of the "Mona Rehab." One day when I was walking with three other friends, we came upon a faucet on the landing of the recreational building. I turned it on so that we could get our hands wet, but instead of turning it off, I turned it up and could not turn it off. The opening of the faucet faced upward, so water started spouting like a fountain. Eventually, an adult came to our rescue. I can't recall whether it was a man or a woman, but we were taken to the matron on duty, who was very upset with me. I was soaking wet from all my efforts to turn the faucet off. The matron wanted to ensure that I did not go out for the rest of the afternoon, so she gave me a big old shirt to put on, and that made me sad. This happened on a beautiful sunny day when the outdoors was warm and inviting.

My grandfather and cousins who lived in the city closer to the center generally came and visited with me, especially on Sundays. On Sundays, men with boxes of ice-cream, popsicles and fudges on the backs of their motorbikes frequently came to the center. My grandfather would usually treat my friends and me, with something from the fudge-man, as they were

THE FACES OF STRUGGLES SUCH AS CANCERS
ARE ON THE JOURNEY TO GOD'S GLORY!

Alfancena Millicent Barrett

affectionately called. Sometimes I got fudge, sometimes a Popsicle, but my favorite was ice cream cake. Even to this day, whenever I eat ice-cream cake, it takes me back to that moment in time.

My grandfather was tall, dark and handsome. He had a very deep voice and I can still hear his voice calling me "MILLIE." I was very special to him and he made it his responsibility to visit me regularly and checked to make sure everything was going well. It was because of this that my mom felt comfortable about leaving me and going back home to the country. This contributed to the development of my independence, and made it easier for me to come to America on my own, away from family.

At that time "Bonanza" was one of my favorite television series that I watched on a regular basis while at "Mona Rehab." I believed it came on about seven o'clock on Thursday nights. One night, right in the middle of a very exciting episode, the power went out. We were so disappointed and prayed that it would come back on, but it did not. Even as an adult, whenever I see "Bonanza" on television, I watch to see if the episode that I missed when the power went out comes to mind. As mentioned previously, folks often went the extra mile for me. This was not only true of the adults around me, but also the older patients. We were usually served chicken soup with dinner, and I liked a lot of chicken in my cup of soup. Most of the nurses, aides and older patients who assisted with serving would grant my request. Every now and then, there would be a server who was not as generous.

THE FACES OF STRUGGLES SUCH AS CANCERS
ARE ON THE JOURNEY TO GOD'S GLORY!

Alfancena Millicent Barrett

I never forget the meanness of one of the nurses or aides. I had the cast on my leg high above my waist which made me unable to walk. It was midday, which was dinner time for us. There was tea early afternoon and supper in the evening. Our mealtime was modeled from the British custom (Jamaica was colonized by the British before it gained its independence in 1962). I needed to use the bed pan, and asked one of the aides. Back then, nurses wore white with a nurse's hat and aides wore pink tunics with white blouses and a nurse's hat.

Apparently the aide forgot, and after more time had passed, I was not able to hold my bowels any longer. The aide was very upset about this, and she complained as she cleaned me up. I so badly wanted to say to her that it was her fault, but that would have made matters worse, and I was not that brave. I cannot remember if I had my dinner that day which was placed on my bedside table, but I remember taking a nap after that ordeal. When the afternoon nurse who was my friend came I relayed to her what had happened earlier. She was not happy about what had taken place, and I believe she reprimanded that individual.

I was unsure of the date I left Mona Rehabilitation Center, but I finally left and started another chapter of my childhood. I believe it was in November 1967 when I first started to attend Mount Nebo Primary School. I was treated like a princess because of my leg; I was given a whole four to six foot bench so that I could elevate my leg and stretch it out. The teachers treated me very delicately, ensuring that I didn't hurt

THE FACES OF STRUGGLES SUCH AS CANCERS ARE ON THE JOURNEY TO GOD'S GLORY!

Alfancena Millicent Barrett

myself. I do not remember how long that lasted, but I was running, jumping, climbing and prancing like all the other six year olds in no time. I know I must have caused many hearts to leap with fear that I would injure myself, because they saw me as being very frail, I was physically active.

I completed primary school without any major incidents. I was involved in everything, which also resulted in me getting in and out of mischief. When I first started to attend Mount Nebo Primary, it was an all-age school. Children could attend that school until they were teenagers. During my time there, I was able to catch a ball very well, which resulted in me being chosen by the older children to be on their team's baseball. The baseball we played in Jamaica was similar to that which is played in the Unites States, but we used one hand to hit the ball instead of a bat. The children in my age group were never happy when that happened. In April 1972 while I was in my final year of primary school, I became a Christian.

We had guest evangelists from the United States. On this particular day, I was sitting in the second bench from the front, and I did not hear a thing the preacher said. The invitation was given at the end of the sermon and the song "Just As I Am" was sang. I got up and started to sing, then suddenly I had the urge to answer the alter call. I was not sure what was taking place because I was only eleven years old. My mom was singing on the choir and she must have sensed what was going on. I looked up at her and she silently mouth "go ahead." I made the walk all by myself, to the front of the church, and answered the call. I am glad that I did. When I got to the back room for counseling, I could not stop crying, but when I was finished crying I felt different. I went through new members classes and was baptized June 4th, 1972 with ten other young people. It was the largest group of young people to get baptized in the history of our church. The day I returned to school after my baptism, I felt like I was just floating in the air. It was a feeling I had never experience before and, since that day, my life was forever changed.

Auntie Lettie's Memories of My Birth

I was fifteen years old when Millie was born. She was delivered by the neighborhood midwife. The day of her birth, when my sister started having contractions, my mom sent someone to call the midwife. In those days, there were no telephones in our town; therefore, all errands and communications were done by foot and word of mouth. As a result of that, when there was an anxious moment, it appeared as if things took forever. Millie's dad was pacing the hallway when the midwife arrived. When it was time for my sister to deliver, my mom called for the hot water and towels. Shortly after that I could hear Millie's cry. I was anxious to see the baby, but I had to wait for what appeared to be hours.

When the adults finally emerged from the room, they were looking quite sad. The joyous moment suddenly turned into questions of "why," "how" and "what." When I inquired, I was told that Millie's right foot was deformed and unless it was corrected, she may be unable to walk. They made plans to take her to the doctor, but before they did that they decided to schedule her dedication which was performed by our pastor, Reverend Oliver Fraser at the Mount Nebo Baptist Church.

That was really a sad time for the family because Millie was leaving for the hospital and our sister Phyllis was leaving for London, England. Millie spent all of her early years in the Mona Rehabilitation Center at the University of the West Indies. She was loved and cared for by the staff. I was told that, in spite of her physical limitation, she was a happy, healthy and social baby, toddler and child. She was always a joy to have around, and even to this day, she has not change.

Millie has demonstrated to us a model child of God. We all admired her love for God, and love for family. She is deeply rooted in her faith, strength, energy and determination. Millie showed us what God's love can do in our lives if we only believe.

Life as a Teenager

My participation in church activities as a teenager was at a very high level. The only thing that kept me from church was sickness. There were times when I had only one pair of shoes for school and church. I found it a pleasure to clean my shoes for church on Sundays. I became a Sunday School teacher around the age of sixteen. I was a member of the youth fellowship and the youth choir. I regularly attended prayer meetings and

THE FACES OF STRUGGLES SUCH AS CANCERS ARE ON THE JOURNEY TO GOD'S GLORY!

Alfancena Millicent Barrett

bible studies. Those days were very exciting times in my life. We traveled to many places to participate as a choir, as a choral group and bible quiz team to compete with other churches. In the summer, we travelled to other churches in the deep rural areas to work in Vacation Bible School. Those were some of the activities that helped foster my independence and leadership qualities.

I started high school in 1973 and I had to walk about two miles or so. We had so much fun traveling that route daily that it appeared to be just around the corner. We especially loved it during day light savings time when we left home in the dark or by the light of the moon to go to school. I continued to develop my leadership skills as a member of the student council and deputy head girl while in high school. Since grade nine, it seems that all of my close friends were born in December the month of my birth. Only one of us was not a Sagittarian. We are still friends today, and keep in touch except for one member of the group. We are still hoping to reunite with our "long lost friend," Marlene. There was a period after high school when we went our separate ways, and we were out of touch for a while.

In high school, I was well liked by the kitchen staff, so I was able to get lunch even if I did not have lunch money. The ladies and men who maintained the buildings and grounds were my friend too. One day, one of the grounds men told me there was something special about me. He said I always wore a smile on my face. I thanked him and thought nothing of his

THE FACES OF STRUGGLES SUCH AS CANCERS
ARE ON THE JOURNEY TO GOD'S GLORY!

Alfancena Millicent Barrett

observation. One day, one of my friends said to me, "Millicent, you never let anything bother you. You are always smiling." At the time, I did not understand that it was the spirit of God that was indwelling in me that was reflecting outwardly. As a Christian, I conducted my life in a certain manner and others were watching. I was still very young in my walk with God. I was attracted to boys, and boys were attracted to me. But, I was also respected by them. They knew the principles by which I lived. I had two boyfriends while I was in high school. When they wanted to take our friendship to "another level" that was where the friendship would end. In my final year of high school a few of my younger brother's friends were always expressing their love for me, but I never took them seriously. I had fun hanging out with them and on graduation day, they made sure I had my picture taken with them.

I remember looking at myself in the mirror, forming my lips in different ways and deciding which way made me looked prettier. My right leg is about an inch and a half shorter than my left leg as a result of the corrective surgery. I would either tiptoe on my right toes or lower my left leg so that I would appear to stand evenly on my legs. Then I would say to myself, "I do have a great shape with my legs even." One day while I was going through this routine, I came to accept the fact that God allowed my leg to be uneven in order to make me humble. A part of the conversation I had with myself was: "Can you image me with such great skin tone, a great shape, and long hair. There is no telling who I would be." As I matured in my Christianity, I understood that it had to be the Holy Spirit. What ordinary teenager would be so accepting of such deformity?

CHAPTER 2

THE FAMILY WHO HELPED TO SHAPE ME

My Mom

My mom, Roslyn Beatrice Chambers, was the first born child to her parents. Her dad died when she was still a young child. Her mother remarried and through that union was blessed with five sisters and two brothers. My mom grew up believing that she had not been given a middle name, however, when she obtained her birth certificate to accompany her passport application, she discovered she had one. For as long as I can remember, my mom's face was always graced by a beautiful smile. At times, we kids would ask, "Mama, what are you smiling about," and she would look at us lovingly and display an even bigger smile.

She often shared her childhood with us in bits and pieces. Because my mom was the eldest child in her family, this made things rough for her at times. She had to do a few chores before going to school in the morning. Some of the life stories that she shared with us were painful for her to talk about. She recounted the morning when one of her brothers was abusive towards her. As she was coming from the river with a tub of clothes on her head, her brother hurled a big stone which hit her in the back. She was really hurt both physically and emotionally by his actions. As the eldest child, she had been given permission to discipline her younger siblings.

THE FACES OF STRUGGLES SUCH AS CANCERS
ARE ON THE JOURNEY TO GOD'S GLORY!

Alfancena Millicent Barrett

Since she had disciplined this particular brother earlier, his abusive actions appeared to have been motivated by his desire to get revenge.

One of my mother's greatest disappointments was that she did not have an opportunity to receive a sound education. Her repeated requests to be educated were ignored. She was able to convince one of her aunts to plead her case to attend vocational school; however, because money was scarce, those efforts were in vain. When mom's dad died, he left the family a well-stocked grocery store, land and cows. Because of this, my mom felt that her mother had the means to provide for her education. Needless to say, her lack of an education was a big disappointment for her, and she made it her life's duty to ensure that her children were educated. My mom taught me how to read, and she required me to read before going to bed each night. During my nightly readings, mispronounced words resulted in my fingers being tapped with a ruler. It was not long before I was reading fluently, and the finger tapping was discontinued.

My mom and dad argued frequently about my brothers abandoning their work in the fields to attend school on Fridays. My mom's motto was "education was the way out of poverty," and she was going to ensure that her children lived by that principle. While we were not rich, we did live well above the poverty line. One thing for sure, though, is that I am very rich with the love and gifts that were bestowed upon me by my mother. It was because of her love for me and others around me that I am the woman that I am today.

THE FACES OF STRUGGLES SUCH AS CANCERS
ARE ON THE JOURNEY TO GOD'S GLORY!

Alfancena Millicent Barrett

My mom, who had been a Christian all of her life, got married at the age of twenty-nine, and had her first child at the age of thirty. Although she was teased by her younger sisters who were single parents, she vowed to not have any children out of wedlock. Looking from the outside in, I had the perfect family structure: mom, dad and siblings. However, towards the end of our teenage years, mom started hinting that things were not all that great between our dad and her. As young adults, we learnt more about her unhappiness, and it made me realize how much of her happiness had been sacrificed for us. My dad was a nag when he was home but, as children, we made fun of some of the rhetoric. At the time, we did not understand the pain that these encounters caused for our mom. She shared with us the fact that she had been unhappy the day after she married. The sad part about it though, was that our dad worked very hard to win her over. Because that love we received from our mother was given so abundantly, we children had no idea that she was experiencing much pain. We only saw her strengths, and how hard she worked to provide us with a better life. I know now that she was able to do that only through God's grace and mercy.

Her service at church meant everything to her, and she always witnessed to others every chance she got. She prayed that all her children would accept Jesus as their Lord and Savior. In her last days, after she was diagnosed with esophagus cancer, she began to have doubts. I was blessed to have had the opportunity to spend two weeks with her in February

THE FACES OF STRUGGLES SUCH AS CANCERS ARE ON THE JOURNEY TO GOD'S GLORY!

Alfancena Millicent Barrett

2003, five months before she passed away. That opportunity was made possible by some of my sisters in Christ at my home church. Before passing, mom expressed feeling guilty about marrying someone who was not a Christian at the time of marriage. My dad subsequently became a Christian. It was sad for me to listen to mom, who I know was the most faithful person, expressed doubts that her sins were not forgiven. I came to believe that God made the trip in February possible because He wanted me to have that precious time with my mom as she was nearing the end of her life on earth.

I was not planning to be in Jamaica at that point in time, but on this particular Sunday at church, I started to cry and could not stop. I went outside and the tears kept flowing. One of my sisters in Christ came to comfort me and to find out what was wrong. I was not even sure myself, but I shared with her the fact that my mom was sick and wasn't able to pay her a visit. Unbeknownst to her, I did not have enough money to go to Jamaica, and I was Concerned about having to take off from work after having been sick for awhile. She suggested that I determine the cost to travel to Jamaica, and confirm my ability to take time off from work. Later that evening, I received a phone call from another one of my sisters in Christ telling me that she had heard about my desire to go home, and extending her offer to purchase my airline ticket. She assured me that she would join with my other sister to sponsor my trip home. At that time, all I could do was give God thanks.

THE FACES OF STRUGGLES SUCH AS CANCERS
ARE ON THE JOURNEY TO GOD'S GLORY!

Alfancena Millicent Barrett

Just prior to my trip for Jamaica, the focus of our Bible Study lesson was "Discipleship." I learned a lot during that time, and was glad that I took my book with me to Jamaica. Those two weeks with my mom were spent studying the bible and praying. I told my mom not to worry about what went wrong, but to pray for all of her children. Even though my return to the United States was difficult, I felt very good because I left feeling confident that my mother's faith was no longer wavering. In fact, I feel certain that her faith had been strengthened.

My Dad

My dad who was very handsome was born in Cuba of Jamaican parentage. He was part Irish and, as a Youngman, he was being "chased" by many "girls." Although mom shared stories of infidelity, we, children, never witnessed this. Growing up, I saw my dad as being very mean-spirited. We called him "Mack-A-Saw," which was a name also given to mom's strict step-father. We kids would call him that name behind his back. We eventually dropped the "Mack-A" and called him "Saw" the name by which he was affectionately called until the day he died.

My dad was a nagger and we were glad when he was not at home. I remember being terrified the first time my mom left home for an overnight trip to the market to sell farm produce. On that night, I saw my dad in a different light. I saw his gentleness as he prepared a meal of fluffy white rice and cow's liver for dinner. That meal smelled and tasted so good that just writing about it, conjures up sweet memories. Before going to bed that night he had devotion with us and I'll never forget how he sang his rendition of the hymn "Man of Sorrow." Another one of my dad's favorite hymns was "Leaning on the Everlasting Arms."

My mom said that my dad nagged only when she was around and, sadly to say, I had to agree with her. We always had to be on our p's and q's when my dad was around, always busy and never playing. He was a great provider who did not approve of me walking around barefooted, probably because of his concern about the problems that I had in prior years with my right leg and foot. He knew that the healing process could take a while. On the other hand he did not have a problem with my brothers going to school barefooted. I was the third of five children and the first girl. So, I had my dad's attention until my sister came along six years later. He was over protective of me, and would not let me carry water from the stand pipe in the community with my brothers. When I was older, he allowed me to go, but I was only allowed to carry a very small container. That was our primary means of accessing water until such time that waterlines were installed in our home. Because he did not allow me go to the fields with my brothers either, they learned to swim and I did not.

As a teenager who had graduated from high school, my dad gave me a hard time. He had a problem with me sleeping late even though I had nowhere to go and there were no major chores to be done. The house

THE FACES OF STRUGGLES SUCH AS CANCERS
ARE ON THE JOURNEY TO GOD'S GLORY!

Alfancena Millicent Barrett

would be clean, clothes washed and ironed, but he still required that I rise up early. He was an early riser who generally went to the fields to check on the cows. One morning upon his return from the fields and finding me still in bed, he asked, "Is miss Queen not up yet?" I never understood why, but he did not like it when I looked directly into his eyes.

When it was time for me to go off to teacher's college and I had to look to him for financial support, the response was very unfavorable. He would eventually give me the money, but he made sure that I knew that he was giving it to me with a heavy heart. Because of the recurring arguments that my dad inflicted upon my mom, I vowed to never let a man treat me like that. Those encounters instilled in me the need to be independent.

I came to learn that overall, my dad was a good person but, he had a difficult time showing affection. I became closer to my dad as a young adult, because we were able to talk about the things that he had said and done in the past. As adults, my siblings and I were able to talk and laugh about many of the things that we experienced growing up, including our dad's disposition. Whenever I returned home for a visit, my dad was always so happy to see me. He would go out of his way to purchase the ingredients to prepare my favorite meals. He also stocked up on a variety of fruits for me.

One of my last memorable moments with my dad was after the funeral for my elder brother. Surrounded by aunts, cousins and my dad, I started talking about my struggles with cancers. My dad said very proudly that nothing had ever stopped me, as he reflected on how determined I was as a child with a leg and foot brace, to overcome the challenges that were placed in front of me. He acknowledged how I ran, climbed and danced in spite of my impediment.

I came to the conclusion that my dad really did love my mom, but did not know how to express his love and affection towards her. Whenever she left home to visit the U.S., she always returned home to home improvement that he knew would please her. He was always happy to see her but, after a few days, he would resort back to his normal grumpy disposition. My dad, who was eighty-four years old when he died of a stroke caused by a cancerous brain tumor, had been working in the fields just five weeks before his death. As my siblings and I reflect on who we are today, we're comforted knowing that we had a good father who had good intentions. His sternness only made us better persons, and we were able to find peace and understanding, as we reconciled the childhood differences that we had with him. In our district, many people thought he was a "rich" man because of the way that he carried himself, and the manner in which we were required to present ourselves in public. He did not possess monetary riches but, he was rich in the way in which he was loved and respected in our community. In spite of the recurring conflicts over the years between the two of us, I must admit that I am glad that he was my dad.

THE FACES OF STRUGGLES SUCH AS CANCERS
ARE ON THE JOURNEY TO GOD'S GLORY!

Alfancena Millicent Barrett

Villair, My Bigger Brother

Villair was the first child born to my mom and dad. Although my dad had two sons before he married my mom, they did not grow up with us. Being the firstborn Villair was the only one of my parents' children who had been photographed as a baby. He was a very quiet child and, even as an adult he was a man of few words. As a teenager, Villair was responsible for taking care of us on the weekends whenever our parents went to the market. One Saturday after Christmas, adorned in the sunglasses which were included among our gifts; we watched the sun rise. Because we lingered so long watching the sun rise, high up in the sky, when Villair called us for breakfast that morning, the fried dumplings and mint tea were cold. We didn't have the heart to complain, so we ate the meal cold. Villair usually prepare our meals and, my brother Cleve would wash the dishes.

Students attending primary or all-age schools were required to take an examination to determine whether or not they would be admitted to high school or a secondary school, which was an alternative high school. Villair was the only of my parents' five children to pass the examination to enter high school. While my other siblings and I were certainly smart enough to attend, it was not God's plan for us to do so. Villair had to travel quite a distance on the big country bus to reach the high school, which required him to rise up very early in the morning. His schedule left very little time for us to spend together. He would leave very early and arrive home with

THE FACES OF STRUGGLES SUCH AS CANCERS
ARE ON THE JOURNEY TO GOD'S GLORY!

Alfancena Millicent Barrett

just enough time to have dinner, do his homework and go to bed. After high school, he went on to pursue his tertiary education. My other siblings and I experienced a break of a year or two before going on to college. I was always happy to see Villair when he came home from college on weekends and holidays.

After graduated from college, Villair accepted a job quite a distance from home. Shortly thereafter, he met Rose who later became his wife and they were proud parents of four beautiful children. His eldest, who was mom's first grandchild, spent a great deal of time with us, away from his parents. I became his main caregiver which led some to believe that I was his mom. One of my friends in Florida was told that I had mothered a baby.

I was very excited to be visited by Villair while I was in college. Oftentimes he arrived with care package for me, and always gave me pocket money before he left. He provided well for our parents needs, and was such an easy going person. Villair and I got along very well; however, there was sadness in his life. He had a weakness for alcohol which in our human minds resulted in his early death. By the time the family became aware of his alcohol addiction, he was too far gone. He tried so hard to quit, but in the process of trying, God called him home.

Our final moments together were pleasant ones, which I will never forget. He had come to visit his son and me in the U.S. While here, he tidied up my yard and fixed a broken light in my kitchen, which had been broken for awhile. Every morning, rain or shine he showed up to prepare me with a cooked meal for my lunch. This was so special to me, because he was actually staying with his son who lived on the next street over from my street. He would leave his son's home in time to arrive at my house by six o'clock in the morning. He was all too happy to do this for me, because the morning before he returned to Jamaica, it was raining heavily, I told him not to bother coming. I could not dissuade him from coming to prepare my meal.

On his departure at the airport, I gave him a warm hug, and took pictures. Little did I know that this would be the last time that we would hug one another. He died the following year. Had I known then that we were hugging one another for the last time; I would have hugged him tighter and longer. The future is not ours to see, so I've learned to live my life each day as if it is the last day. "Villair, my beloved brother rest in peace until we meet again." I remember his kindness and concern for others. He offered me a great deal of encouragement in my life pursuits. I miss Villair so much.

Cleve, My Big Brother

Cleve who bears a strong resemblance to me, is dark complexion, like me. We were close in birth, being only a year and five months apart. We also shared a close friendship until we had a big break up as young adults. Cleve was two years younger than Villair, while I was two years older

Alfancena Millicent Barrett

than my youngest brother Lambert, and six years older than my only sister, Reita.

Growing up, Cleve and my other siblings and I were always getting into fights on Saturdays when our parents were away from home. Most of the time, it was Villair, Lambert and I against Cleve but, once in awhile, we would gang up against Villair. I can't recall the specific reasons for the fights but, as we were growing up, Cleve tended to be a daring child. One Saturday, Cleve was chasing us down the hill with a stool, and a neighbor stopped him to ask if he was crazy. The fighting would eventually come to an end and then we'd end up chatting and laughing as though nothing had happened. Because of Cleve's daring nature, our dad found it necessary to discipline him with a stronger hand.

When Cleve became a teenager and refused to be disciplined in the manner which had been used when he was younger, my dad had to abandon that form of disciplining. On one occasion, my dad spanked me and Cleve intervened, because he felt that this was unfair punishment. After a school trip, I went with some friends to another town. Unbeknownst to me, one of the girls in the group had a crush on the van driver. In a jealous rage, she poisoned herself and ended up in the hospital. A few weeks later my dad learned about the incident and that I had gone on the trip. True to form, my dad did not ask any questions in order to hear my side of the story. Instead, he proceeded to discipline me. I saw Cleve as my hero that day, because had he not intervened, it's difficult to say

Alfancena Millicent Barrett

what the end result might have been.

Cleve was also very adventurous. He would tell us some of the things that he did and the places that he frequented when he should have been in school. When he was in the eighth grade and was not reading at grade level, my mom made a trip to school to talk with the principal. The principal's investigation revealed that Cleve had been absent from classes on several occasions. Cleve was disciplined by the principal, and this provided to be a turning point for him. From that point on, he did what he was supposed to do in school and when he transferred to the ninth grade he was among the top students in the class. I was really impressed with the progress he made in such a short time. That made me realize just how capable Cleve was. My mom was not going to stand by and let her son be denied the education that he deserved. Cleve was very grateful for all that she did and he eventually pursued a career as a professional teacher.

In Jamaica, our native language is English (the Queen's English), but we speak Creole (patois) which is a broken English with a French dialect. Cleve was always correcting my English, especially my pronunciation of certain words. He always had to correct my pronunciation of the word "film" (fil′m). To this day, I have to pause before saying that word. Cleve has two daughters who speak almost perfect English. I believe, they were trained by my brother, Cleve, to master the language at a very early age.

Cleve and I who shared an apartment after college had a lot of disagreements as young adults. Our differences often started with the women in his life and the way he treated them. I expected him to treat women the way I wanted to be treated and, often times he did not. So whenever I confronted him about his disrespectful behavior, he and I would have a falling out. The last squabble that we had ended with me moving out. Because of that, we did not speak to one another for a long time.

Our reconciliation was my first real test of forgiveness. When I decided to forgive my brother, Cleve, my whole body ached and it really took a lot out of me. I was weakened physically by that experience. In the end, I gained spiritual strength. Up until now, I had never shared those feelings with anyone. That experience made it easier for me to forgive others who hurt me along the way. I have learned how to tell people instantly or shortly thereafter how their behavior affected me, and then move on from the hurt. I have even reached out to individuals who have slighted me, all in the spirit of forgiveness.

My brother Cleve helped me to understand what Jesus taught us about forgiveness. I am happy that God has spared my life to see him celebrate his fiftieth birthday. I pray that he will be in service for God.

Lambert, My Little Brother

Lambert who is two years younger than I, did not do well with Villair's late morning breakfasts. One Saturday, he became ill after eating breakfast, which resulted in our dad having to come home from the market

THE FACES OF STRUGGLES SUCH AS CANCERS
ARE ON THE JOURNEY TO GOD'S GLORY!

Alfancena Millicent Barrett

to take him to the dispenser at the drug store. He was the only medical personnel who were accessible on weekends in our rural town. Lambert's appetite was not very good prior to that incident; however, after taking the medication that was dispensed from the drug store, his appetite improved tremendously.

Lambert and I played together a lot when we were children. During our play time we tended to favor mud and leaves. I emulated Lambert, and became a "tomboy." Some of our favorite games were cricket, rolling down hills, climbing trees and going down hills on a coconut bunker (main vain of the coconut tree leaf). This was similar to sliding down a snowy hill on a sled.

Lambert was very "smooth" with the girls at an early age. When he was in the fourth grade he was reprimanded for verbalizing the fact that he had a crush on his teacher. She was not impressed with his openness, and told our dad about it, who proceeded to spank him. In my opinion that spanking only encouraged him more, because he continued to be a "lady's man" and many of the women who he befriended, were much older than he. The day that Lambert called me to announce his plan to get married, I was shocked. I didn't think that I would live to see the day when he made a commitment to a woman.

When Lambert became a Christian, we all thought that he had a promising future as a minister of the gospel. He knew how to prepare a sermon, and his delivery was very impressive. After awhile, his sermons didn't have the same affect on me as they did in the beginning. I believe that it was six sense that suggested to me that something wrong. One day, Lambert said he did not want to serve as a minister anymore. In expressing his feelings, he literally picked up the bible and placed it on the floor. He did eventually leave the fellowship of the church. Lambert became weakened and distracted by the good time that he was having partying and by all the girls who were at his beck and call. He later turned from those ways and recommitted his life to Jesus Christ. That was a was a happy day for the family.

My brother is a very proud individual. There was a time when I thought he was mean-spirited because of something that he had done when we were children. One day, one of our neighborhood elders gave him two oranges, and I asked him if I could have one. He refused to share one with me and, when I pressed him, he tossed both oranges in the gully (valley) on our way home. I never understood the meaning of his actions, but I remember being hurt by them, and my inability to forget that incident.

As adults, we had disagreements with one another. We went through an extended period of not speaking to one another after I refused his request for a loan. I found it very difficult to say no; but, after examining the situation further, I decided to "stick to my guns." That experience made me realize that it was okay to say "no" even to someone you love. Since that day, I have never hesitated to say "no" after examining a situation when it did not feel like the right thing to do. The impact that my

THE FACES OF STRUGGLES SUCH AS CANCERS
ARE ON THE JOURNEY TO GOD'S GLORY!

Alfancena Millicent Barrett

younger brother Lambert has had on me has helped to mold the person I am today.

Lambert's Personal Memories and Expressions

From an early age, I knew my sister as an active child, even though she walked with a limp and had a big scar on one of her leg. I was told that her leg was bent during child birth, and the doctors had to implant a piece of iron in it to keep it straight. At times, we teased her by calling her "iron foot", but she kept her cool and never reacted. I can still remember the foot brace with the thick base shoe attached to it, lying in our backyard after she had outgrown it. It then became one of our favorite toys. Millie, as she was affectionately known, had long black hair. I can still remember how she always cried whenever our mom combed it. We, as brothers, would sit close by and help to comfort her by counting down the number of braids that were yet to be done by saying, "Three more bawling left Millie."

As a teenager, she continued to be very active and very much involved. She was faced with her fair share of teenage challenges, including the crushes that she had on boys and those that the boys had on her. During her final year of secondary school, a college guy from a neighboring district, at the time, approached me close to our home to enquire about a girl who he had come to like. He wanted to know exactly where she lived so that he could see her. He started describing her to me:

THE FACES OF STRUGGLES SUCH AS CANCERS ARE ON THE JOURNEY TO GOD'S GLORY!

Alfancena Millicent Barrett

deputy head girl at the secondary school; dark complexion with long black hair and bright eyes; and she walked with a limp. I laughed out loud and told him that the girl that he had just described was my sister Millicent. We both burst into laughter at that revelation.

Millicent was the first one in the family to leave home. Her living in the United States was a big thing to the rest of us. I can still remember the pictures of her first winter there, playing in and shoveling the snow. This was something that none of us had ever experienced. Millicent loves children, so I thought that she would be the first to get marry and have lots of kids. I could never understand why, but our dad would become very upset whenever we were at church and Millicent would show up with someone's baby or child in her arms.

After several failed relationships, we received word that Millicent was getting married. Unfortunately, at the time, only Villair, my late elder brother, had a United States visa, and could attend the wedding. We were all very happy for her. For a period of time, everything: her marriage; her studies; and her job, was going well for her. Then came the sad news that Millicent had developed cancer in her lungs.

I questioned how that could be possible, because she never smoked or lived with anyone who did. The treatments went well as did her recovery. Then, the "bottom fell out." She was diagnosed with breast cancer, and was having marital problems, which eventually led to her divorce. A short time later, she was diagnosed with uterine cancer, and then a reoccurrence

THE FACES OF STRUGGLES SUCH AS CANCERS
ARE ON THE JOURNEY TO GOD'S GLORY!

Alfancena Millicent Barrett

of lymphoma. In spite of all of these major setbacks, one could not look at her or talk to her on the phone and know that she was facing such enormous life challenges. She remained upbeat, and would always greet everyone with a big smile. She was always concerned about how others felt about her health challenges, and would often spend time trying to cheer them up.

When I called to find out how she was doing she would answer the phone with so much excitement and enthusiasm. She would tell me about the tomatoes she had picked, and the calalu (dark green leafy vegetable) that she had cut from her vegetable garden. She was also eager to tell me about pretty dresses that she had bought for my daughter. Even after all of her recurring bouts with cancers she kept busy attending to her garden, changing door locks, washing her car, hosting parties, and staying in touch with family and friends. Millicent has always been good about remembering birthdays and anniversaries, and you could always count on her to call on that special day. Her ability to "connect" with others and to stay in touch had been perfected long before the launching of "Facebook". After the deaths of our elder brother Villair and his wife, Millicent decided to pursue the adoption of Junior, our nephew who is a functioning Down Syndrome child. I told her that she was in no shape to care for a child; much less a special needs child. She just smiled and said that, with God's help, she would manage.

Her strong faith in God propelled her through all of her ordeals, and I

THE FACES OF STRUGGLES SUCH AS CANCERS
ARE ON THE JOURNEY TO GOD'S GLORY!

Alfancena Millicent Barrett

still marvel at her strength and courage. Long after Millicent had her first bout with cancer, we lost several family members to cancer. They are long gone, while she is still here to tell her story.

Cancer is not robbing her of a full and productive life. Instead, she is actually thriving. If I survive her, my dream is to grow up and be just like her. Like Millicent, my desire is to have the outlook on life, and despite the odds, live by faith in God. She is my **HERO.**

Reita (Peaches) My Only Sister

Peaches were born six years after I, and I really enjoyed assisting with her care as she was growing up. I wiped the tears from her eyes when she cried because, as her elder sister, I never wanted to see her cry. I would comb her hair and took great care to ensure that her braids were adorned by ribbons, even though at times, her ribbons were concocted from leftover material from our mom's sewing box. Nevertheless, I was always pleased with how pretty she was after I had finished combing her hair.

One day while Peaches was in preschool (basic school), I found myself in "hot water" because I decided to leave class to spend the afternoon with her at her school which was adjacent to the school that I attended. I was hoping that the teacher would not miss me; however, the next morning I learned my fate. It just so happened that, on the day that I left school, most of the girls in my class had decided to skip class too. They spent the whole afternoon playing on a playground which we called "common". Our

THE FACES OF STRUGGLES SUCH AS CANCERS
ARE ON THE JOURNEY TO GOD'S GLORY!

Alfancena Millicent Barrett

teacher was a strong disciplinarian who did not believe in "sparing the rod". She lined us all up and whipped us before we could enter the classroom. In those days it was not unusual for children to be whipped in school for misbehaving. No doubt, this contributed to our willingness to take a break from her class that bright sunny afternoon. In spite of my misfortune, I had no regrets from having spent the afternoon with my baby sister.

Once she was able to talk Peaches became our dad's confidant. My dad would get her anything she desired, especially cheese and homemade crackers. Sometimes she would eat this instead of her dinner. Whenever our dad returned home from outside the house Peaches would report on everything that the others had done. I can recall a time when the "tables were turned" on Peaches. Shortly after new steps had been constructed at the entrance to our verandah, Peaches "having fun", decided to take a machete and cut the edges of the steps. My elder brother, knowing that her actions spelled t-r-o-u-b-l-e, established a plan to get revenge for something that Peaches had done to him previously. He told Peaches to tell our dad that he was responsible for the damage which had been done to the steps. Our dad did not believe her, and demanded to know the truth. She eventually confessed that she had been responsible for the damaged steps, which resulted in her being whipped by our dad. We all felt so sorry for her, especially my elder brother who had encouraged her to tell the lie.

My Early Childhood Development and Human Behavior studies in

THE FACES OF STRUGGLES SUCH AS CANCERS
ARE ON THE JOURNEY TO GOD'S GLORY!

Alfancena Millicent Barrett

college led me to believe that Peaches' life changed after that whipping. I believe the thought of Peaches being punished for her actions affected the choices that she made throughout her life. As I reflect on my sister's life from that day on, memories comes to mind. Peaches would oftentimes relate stories that were believable but which were, in fact, all fiction. The men she chose tended to be selfish and uncaring towards her. She never took an interest in the ones who were caring and protective of her. Tears come to my eyes as I write about this incident that took place in Peaches' life that I believe contributed to her struggles. She was about three or four years old when it took place. The first man she trusted, our dad, hurt her for relating the version instructed by our elder brother about who was responsible for damaging the steps at the entrance of the veranda. In spite of her struggles, she is one of the sweetest persons I know. She is kind and has a personality that naturally draws people to her. She is oftentimes willing to take care of other people's needs before, taking care of her own. This was also one of my mother's strongest attributes.

Growing up with my sister Peaches made me realize that I am not a jealous person. I've always wanted the best for other people regardless of who they were. Our friends would often say that my sister was prettier than I, however, this never affected me in a negative way. One day, I decided to reinforce the notion that "beauty is only skin deep" by responding that Peaches is pretty on the outside, while I am pretty on the inside. I did not at the time really understand what I was saying, because at

THE FACES OF STRUGGLES SUCH AS CANCERS
ARE ON THE JOURNEY TO GOD'S GLORY!

Alfancena Millicent Barrett

the time I was just saying words. I now understand that when a person is filled with the "Spirit of God" within, that "Spirit" tends to glow outward. Peaches also taught me patience. She would sometimes wear the clothes that I reserved for special occasions to her work. This would make me really angry; however I learned how to handle my anger and love her at the same time.

Peaches had a beautiful singing voice. My hope was that she would use that talent to define the person that she had become. I always thought she could have been a great gospel singer; however, that was my dream. She had her own dreams, and I love her all the same.

I was blessed to be a part of such a wonderful family who contributed so much to the person who I am today. I did not realize how much they had impacted my life until I took time out to reflect on who I am. My family members often talked about the strength that they observed in me, however, I am strong because of God's grace and mercy, and the family that helped to shape me and my life.

CHAPTER 3

COLLEGE AND EARLY ADULTHOOD

At some point in my life, I decided that I wanted to become either a nurse or a teacher. In my country, there were more colleges to train teachers than there were nursing schools. Because of the amount of time that I spent in the hospital, I always thought that I would become a nurse. I eventually concluded that, because I would have a difficult time administering injections, I would pursue a teaching career instead of nursing. The two years between high school and heading off to college were the most miserable years because of my dad's nagging ways.

He seemed to do everything to "drive me crazy" but through it all I became stronger and more determined. As mentioned earlier my dad was not fond of my habit of sleeping in. On one of those days when he commented about this, I asked myself, "What is wrong with that man?" I had nowhere to go, and all my house chores were completed. I oftentimes wondered about his motives and at times I just cried.

I eventually applied to several colleges. I was accepted by one of the catholic colleges in Kingston, Jamaica and started making preparation to leave home and my nagging Dad.

Before I left for college, I received a beautiful white and gold Christmas card from a secret admirer. I had no idea who it was from, and because there was no return address, I had no way of finding out. So, I went off to college in September 1980 without solving that mystery. When I came home to visit on Valentine's Day, I received another card but this time my secret admirer revealed himself. It was really a surprise because he was only an occasional visitor to our district. We became very good friends, and our friendship continues today. He asked my dad's permission for us to enter into "courtship". As excited as I was that day, I remember going outside while he talked with my dad. My brother Cleve decided to hang around to eavesdrop. We had a beautiful relationship and were certain that we would eventually marry; however, when he came to the United States to accept employment, things went sour. We parted company for a while, and reunited a few times; however, in spite of our great friendship, we never married. I have come to accept the fact that marrying him was not part of God's divine plan for me.

The relationship between my dad and me improved after leaving home for college. Life at college was enlightening and interesting. My time there provided me with the opportunity to build a social network of people from very diverse backgrounds. I was fascinated one day when one of the gardeners stopped me and said, "You are always smiling," which reminded me of my high school days when others commented the same way. I still hear those same words today from many of my associates.

The college that I attended gave me the opportunity to continue my walk with God. Every Friday morning we were allowed to assemble with

THE FACES OF STRUGGLES SUCH AS CANCERS
ARE ON THE JOURNEY TO GOD'S GLORY!

Alfancena Millicent Barrett

others who were of the same religious denomination. There were times though, when we joined together for interdenominational sessions. I was, at one time the president of the Baptist group. I was able to accept that role, and performed well because of the leadership qualities I developed as a member of the youth fellowship group at my childhood church, Mount Nebo Baptist.

I was also a vibrant sports participant. I participated in college track and field events. I also had a passion for netball, and at one point in time, I was the team captain. As a part of the college netball team I had the opportunity to travel to parts of Jamaica that I had never visited before college. I developed many skills in college that aided me throughout my career and life, in general. College taught me to be resourceful and creative. We had to prepare teaching materials in all subject areas in preparation for our practice teaching sessions. We labeled ourselves as "trash collectors" because we learnt how to convert "trash" into treasured material to help enhance children's learning and development. We were graded for creativity and usability. Once a week, we would hit the streets to travel to printing factories and supermarkets in search of boxes and paper scrap. We did in all good fun. Sometimes we worked as a team and at other times, we worked individually. Either way, we had a lot of fun serving as "trash collectors".

In fulfillment of my one year long of internship, I was assigned a classroom of five year olds. It was a very small space for a little but less

THE FACES OF STRUGGLES SUCH AS CANCERS
ARE ON THE JOURNEY TO GOD'S GLORY!

Alfancena Millicent Barrett

than twenty students. I was challenged with making that space attractive for learning, and did better than I thought I would. The group of children that was assigned to me was very eager to learn and performed very well by the end of the school year. For some reason, the principal, at the school where I did my internship, had it in for me. She had to evaluate me and it seemed as though I could do nothing right by her. Although she did so with a smile, she would give me marginal grades for almost everything that I did. Some of the same materials that she graded as being marginal were afforded higher grades by my college supervisor, who did not realize that the materials had already been graded. Her negative attitude towards me made me realize that I was a graceful person. In spite of her demeanor towards me I always returned the smile and never revealed my disgust and disappointment with her. Because of this relationship I was doubtful about my prospects of being extended a job offer at that school upon completion of my teaching internship. Even if an employment offer had been made, I don't believe I would have accepted it.

With maturity, I have come to realize that in life, God allows us to experience disappointments in order to prepare us to serve Him better.

My First Job

As a young person in my country, when one leaves the rural area and head off to college, the plan is not to return home. My desire was not to go to live in another rural area, but it was getting close to the start of a new

THE FACES OF STRUGGLES SUCH AS CANCERS
ARE ON THE JOURNEY TO GOD'S GLORY!

Alfancena Millicent Barrett

school year and I had not received any responses from the job applications I sent out to public and private schools. On this particular day, I felt a little down, so I took a nap. Shortly thereafter, I was awoken by the phone. When I answered, the caller identified herself as the principal from one of the private schools to which I had sent a job application. She confirmed receipt of my application, but needed some additional information from me. Much to my amazement, I was extended a offer without being scheduled for an interview. I agreed to get back to her ASAP with the requested information. I immediately arose. I proceeded to gather the documents and responded the same day rather than waiting until the next day.

In September 1983 I officially started my teaching career. It was a great job. My class consisted of a group of twenty-five (25) five years old. This was one of the best group of children that I had the privilege to teach throughout my teaching career. By the end of the school year, some of the children were reading at a grade two level. This level of my success and achievement proved to be quite impressive to my principal and co-workers. I found it difficult to take credit for this accomplishment because the children were so eager to learn. I took credit for having created an attractive learning environment. Because of my first year achievements, I was assigned responsibility for working with children who were performing below grade level. It was always a great feeling to reach the end of a school year, and observe children excelling in areas where they

THE FACES OF STRUGGLES SUCH AS CANCERS
ARE ON THE JOURNEY TO GOD'S GLORY!

Alfancena Millicent Barrett

had been deficient. I not only had a strong bond with the children, but I also bonded well with the parents. I taught at that school for six years. It was truly a "labor of love".

I had the urge to move on, and was drawn to the public school environment, even though it had less classroom space, and more children. At one point in time, I had sixty children mainly boys, in one class. This situation hindered my effectiveness and, consequently, I did not remain in this teaching role for the full year. By this time, I had experience working with children from first grade through six grade. Over the years, I started to encounter children in the higher grades who were not very interested in their education. Although that made my job difficult, I was always pleased with the progress that most of the children made by the end of the school year. At that particular school, there was a football (soccer) field that had a dirt surface which resulted in a very dusty environment. Usually by Wednesday of each week, I would become ill, and experience hoarseness. I found myself having to visit the Ear, Nose and Throat (ENT) doctor very often. I worked at that facility for three years, and when I was extended the opportunity to relocate to the United States, that unhealthy work environment made it easy for me to accept the offer.

I hated having to leave the family of workers I had came to know and love. I loved the sincere fellowship among the staff members. It was like one big support group. When a staff member lost a loved one, the group's support would be very obvious at the funeral service. There was a great

THE FACES OF STRUGGLES SUCH AS CANCERS
ARE ON THE JOURNEY TO GOD'S GLORY!

Alfancena Millicent Barrett

deal of cooperation extended to one another in working towards the achievement of our goals and objectives, including the fundraising aspects of that program. The funds which were raised enabled us to enjoy some of the finer things in life. Before we left for summer break, the staff would get away to an exotic part of the island for some fun and relaxation. We would also dine, as a group, at one of the finest restaurants or hotels before leaving for Christmas break. These were some of my favorite outings because they afford me the opportunity to dress up and enhance my external beauty! As I reflected on my departure from that job, I did so acknowledging that it was not due to my desire to leave, but rather because of God's need for me to be someplace else.

CHAPTER 4

COMING TO AMERICA

First Visit

One of my cousins who I had met for the first time as an adult made my first visit to the United States possible. He defined me as being his favorite cousin from my parents' offspring and, because of this, he sent me an invitation to his son's graduation. In order for me to accept the invitation, though, I had to apply for a United States visa. I had planned on going to the embassy to pick up the application and to set up an appointment for the interview for a later date. I wanted time to familiarize myself with the application requirements prior to having to go before the interviewer.

I had a dream the night before going to the embassy, and it was an interesting dream. I dreamt that I was walking along and a bee kept buzzing in my ear. Each time I swatted the bee, it came back. I thought about the dream when I woke up, and wondered what it meant. My mom had told me previously that bees signified money. I left home early that morning hoping that, when I arrived at the embassy, the line would not be very long. But, sure enough, it was. I took my place in line and noticed that the person in front of me was an acquaintance. We chatted about a number of things as we waited. I told her that my plan was to pick up the

Alfancena Millicent Barrett

visa application and schedule the appointment for a later date. She suggested that if I were lucky enough to get an appointment for today, that I should take it. I mentioned that I really wanted to familiarize myself with the questions before the interview. She, again, advised me to accept the appointment if it were scheduled for today. Moving up in the line, she repeated those words to me. After hearing those words for the fourth time, my dream of that nagging bee came to mind.

I had been told some time ago that a person had a better chance of getting a visa if he or she was married, owned a home and had money in the bank. Stable employment was also a consideration, as it served as evidence that one had sufficient ties to Jamaica and therefore, was more likely to return. Ironically, the lady with whom I had conversed while in the line fit this profile; however, she was refused a visa. On the other hand I was single had only worked at my present job for one year and eight months, and didn't have enough money in the bank to buy my plane ticket. When I got up to the window8:45 a.m., I was given a 10:00 a.m. appointment. Although I did not have all of the documents which I had been told were needed, God's divine plan made it possible for me to have most of the documents with me. The most important thing I did not have was the visa picture. As it turned out, my blessings kept on flowing. Visa picture taking was a big business outside of the embassy, and I was able to get my picture taken right then and there. Those pictures were the ugliest that I had ever taken, but there was no need to complain, because I had no

THE FACES OF STRUGGLES SUCH AS CANCERS
ARE ON THE JOURNEY TO GOD'S GLORY!

Alfancena Millicent Barrett

other choice and no time to go elsewhere. As I approached the time for my interview, I became very nervous.

My interviewer was very warm, and she wanted to know the name of the college where the graduation was being held, the name of the graduate, and how long I was planning to stay in the United States. I could not even pronounce the name of the college properly. I told her my plan was to be in the United States for five days, and she warned me not to stay any longer than the five days. I was limited to the five days because this was my vacation entitlement after 20 months on the job. Much to my surprise, I was issued a multiple one-year visa to the United States, which meant that for a year, I could travel back and forth from Jamaica to the United States. My interpretation of all that had transpired is that when God has something in store for you, no one can deny you.

I visited three states in five days. I arrived at J.F.K. Airport on a Friday night and took a connecting flight on a very small plane to Rochester, New York. On Saturday morning, we traveled from Rochester, New York to New Jersey. We spent the night in New Jersey, and headed down to Pennsylvania on Sunday to attend the graduation ceremony. After the graduation ceremony, we traveled to New York City, by way of the Holland Tunnel. I was really fascinated by the fact that the Tunnel could be constructed under the river. I had my picture taken in front of the Empire State Building in Manhattan before heading to Queens, New York. Later that day, traveled back to Rochester, New York.

THE FACES OF STRUGGLES SUCH AS CANCERS
ARE ON THE JOURNEY TO GOD'S GLORY!

Alfancena Millicent Barrett

On Monday, I went shopping with one of my cousins. Another cousin prepared a delicious dinner, but our shopping outing delayed our return, which was upsetting to him. All of this happened the day before my return to Jamaica. After dinner, I learned the real reason for my cousin being so upset. He was planning to take me to Niagara Falls, but had to scrap those plans because it was too late. After learning that, I was very disappointed, because a trip to Niagara Falls would have been "the icing on the cake" for my world-wind trip. My cousin did, eventually, take me to Niagara Falls on one of my return trips to the United States.

I traveled to Miami, Florida for the summer before my visa was expired. I later renewed my visa and was issued a five year multiple visa, which allowed me to travel back and forth for five years. I took full advantage of this privilege. In 1995, I decided to attend school in the United States. I desired a change in my life, and I wanted to see the world. The fact that I kept getting sick at my place of employment did help make up my mind. I was single, childless and feeling adventurous. So, the transition was easy for me to make. Each time I reflect on the move that I made, I'm comforted by the key message of a sermon which was delivered at one the churches I visited shortly after my arrival in Delaware. The message was that "*God does not lead you where He will not provide for you.*" My belief is that I was sent here by God. All of my pursuits in this country were facilitated by the doors which God opened or the people who He placed in my life to provide assistance. In times of need, I had friends

THE FACES OF STRUGGLES SUCH AS CANCERS
ARE ON THE JOURNEY TO GOD'S GLORY!

Alfancena Millicent Barrett

in unexpected places treated me with kindness. While attending school in the United States, I was often asked "*Why are you here instead of in your beautiful home country, Jamaica*?" My usual response was that, "I am here because of the opportunities that this country has to offer." Sometimes I went into much greater detail to explain God's plan for my life, while at other times I was brief in my response.

Answer to the Question, "Why Are You Here?"

My experiences here have further refined my answer to that question. "*I am here because God brought me here for a purpose.*" I received confirmation of this when I reflected on all the lives that I have touched and the ones that have touched mine.

I attended Delaware Technical and Community College (Deltech) for four years and received two Associate Degrees: one in Early Childhood Education, and the other in Human Services. While at Deltech, I became a member of the Peer Associates which afforded me an opportunity to travel to many places outside of the state to represent my college. I was also able to develop skills as a motivational speaker. It was through this group that I met my ex-husband. I vividly remember the day that I met him. We were having "A World Diversity Day", where the map of the world was on the floor of the conference room. I can't recall all of the sessions which were held that day but, at the end of the event, I was introduced to him by the director of our Peer Associates. From that day on, we only saw one

THE FACES OF STRUGGLES SUCH AS CANCERS
ARE ON THE JOURNEY TO GOD'S GLORY!

Alfancena Millicent Barrett

another occasionally. We eventually found out that we had both graduated the same day in 1997, he from Human Services and I from Early Childhood program. In acknowledgement of this common experience, he made me aware that he gave me a hug on the day of graduation. To this day, I can't recall that moment. I must have been in another world!

A few months later, we met in the hallway at college and carried on a lengthy conversation. Before parting company, he gave me his phone number. One Friday evening as I was looking through my books, I found his number and gave him a call. It occurred to me then that I had not given him my number. We engaged in a long conversation and discussed a variety of topics. I found him to be quite interesting, and we became phone buddies. We later progressed to the "friend" stage, which will be covered in more detail in the chapters ahead.

CHAPTER 5

GOD CHOSE SHILOH BAPTIST CHURCH FOR ME

I was living with relatives in the suburb of New Castle, Delaware which made it difficult for me to get to school and work in the city of Wilmington. As He consistently done, the Lord opened doors for me. I was able to get place in the city on my small wages. I was happy that it was located close to a church which was within walking distance, because, at the time, I did not own a car. I did not start attending this church right away because I was working on the weekends. Every time I passed the church my desire to explore the fellowship experience there increased. I found myself really missing being in church on Sundays.

At the time I was working with an elderly woman who was very sick. My hope at the time was that God would help me to lead this woman to have a relationship with Him. She was very bitter about her sickness, and couldn't understand why she ended up in her predicament when many of her friends who practiced the same habits, did not get sick. I was hoping that my treating her with kindness and talking to her about the love of God would made a difference in her life. After awhile, I realized that my leading her to Christ was not God's plan because this woman was a "hard nut to crack", and I was becoming spiritually drained. I realized that I needed refueling for myself before I could be effective in helping someone

THE FACES OF STRUGGLES SUCH AS CANCERS
ARE ON THE JOURNEY TO GOD'S GLORY!

Alfancena Millicent Barrett

like her. I quit the weekend job, and the following weekend I visited Shiloh.

I did not know anyone at the church, but my goal was to meet Jesus. I knew that if I met Jesus there, everything would be just fine. Sure enough, on my first visit, I felt the presence of God and I knew then that was where God wanted me to be. I became a member of the fellowship soon after that first visit and I had not had any regrets. The relatives I lived with when I first came to Delaware had relocated to another state; therefore I had no blood ties in this place. When I became a member of the Shiloh family, I realized I had moms, dads, sisters and brothers. I felt the love of Jesus through those people. I was living the song, "I am so glad I am a part of the family of God!"

In 2000 I was diagnosed with "non-Hodgkin lymphoma cancer." My church family was there for me. I was able to call any member of that family to do anything for me during that time of sickness and it was done. I received cards, phones calls, visits and prayers that went up to God which I felt in my spirit. I went through many battles with the fight against cancer and my church family never complained, they gave me the support I needed. Often times they showed their love for me that went beyond my expectations. Their act of kindness reminded me of my favorite quote; "God does not lead you where He will not provide for you."

The Bible Study sessions that I attended at Shiloh had helped me to grow spiritually and increase my faith. I really missed going to Bible

THE FACES OF STRUGGLES SUCH AS CANCERS
ARE ON THE JOURNEY TO GOD'S GLORY!

Alfancena Millicent Barrett

Study when my health conditions hindered me. On Sundays when I was in church I always recorded the key points from the sermons. I keep them in a special box that I can read and meditate on when I cannot make it to church. It is a blessing when one can feel very comfortable and loved in a church family. I went to Shiloh to meet Jesus and fellowship with God's people and God chose to give me more. I did not go to seek friends; I did not go and wonder what Shiloh had to offer me; my number one goal was to meet Jesus, and I did. As a result of that, I received more than my expectations. My experiences at Shiloh made me understand more clearly the passage of scripture from Matthew 6:33 (KJV) "Seek ye first the Kingdom of God and all things shall be added unto you."

I was a member of a few ministries; some of which, I had to give up when I got sick. I am still an active member of the deaconess and evangelism ministries. Ministries I will continue to serve once my health is restored; there is pleasure in serving Jesus. One of my life long goals is to serve God in whatever I do and wherever I go. I performed better at a job when I do it to please God instead of man. I have discovered that it is so much more rewarding that way, too. I have observed people who worked to please man; how frustrated and anxious they became when something went wrong.

The spiritual teaching I received has really assisted in my Christian maturity. I was able to face each struggle by faith. The struggles I had gone through in my life had taught me what it meant to have Faith. My

THE FACES OF STRUGGLES SUCH AS CANCERS
ARE ON THE JOURNEY TO GOD'S GLORY!

Alfancena Millicent Barrett

experiences had taught me what it meant to trust God completely. When God brought you through one situation there is no reason to doubt he will not bring you out of the next. I do not know if God has something bigger for me to do, but with each struggle I grew stronger. I pray to remain humble and be ready to carry out God's will in my life.

Each individual that God had placed in my life, God used them to help me get further along on the journey. I pray for my Shiloh family that they will continue to live in the will of God and their baskets never be empty. I praise God daily that He allowed me to be a part of such a family. One of my special moments at Shiloh I mentioned earlier was when one of my sisters led the way to make it possible for me to go see my sick mom back home in Jamaica. I could not believe that was happening; this was something that I did not even ask God to do. I guess God needed me to be with my mom at that time and he made it possible. As a result of their kindness, I had the most beautiful two weeks with my mom. We celebrated her seventy-six birthday with a well attended crowd. She died later that year July sixth, 2003. I was unable to be by her side when she went onto glory, but because I had a chance to spend some time with her before her appointed time, I felt very peaceful within my soul. I will ever be grateful for those sisters. There were many more acts of kindness that will be shared as I continue to tell my story.

CHAPTER 6

MARRIAGE AND THE CANCER OF DIVORCE

I had a beautiful wedding day and was looking forward to a beautiful life with my husband. God provided people in my life that gave me a wedding day I did not expect because we did not have much money; no one who witnessed my wedding could have known that. My husband at the time had two children and I was happy they were able to participate in our wedding. We had built a great friendship for two years before we got married. I liked the way we could have talked about every and anything. I was excited because this was someone I could spend the rest of my life with. We were able to deal with conflicts in our friendship and I believed this would work great in our marriage. He was also highly recommended as a good person by friends, that's how it was at first in our marriage, but something changed and we could no longer see things the same.

Our marriage was a workable one. I was a Christian, but my husband was not. I was determine to live my life in order that my husband see Christ in me. My husband, early in our marriage, would share in my daily devotions and our marriage was going fairly well. I believed in my heart that at some point in time he was convicted by the Holy Spirit, but was not willing to return to God's fold. My husband was a Christian who had fallen from grace. He started professing his belief in other religion, which,

THE FACES OF STRUGGLES SUCH AS CANCERS
ARE ON THE JOURNEY TO GOD'S GLORY!

Alfancena Millicent Barrett

I was never sure which one, because sometimes he read book from one religion and soon after he was reading another. His search for answers in those other books did not last long. When I look back, I realized things changed when he would no longer participate in my devotion. During our troubled times I shared with a friend what was going on and the things he was doing and she said to me; "His behavior painted a picture of someone running from God." She confirmed what I was feeling at the time. I asked him one day if when he was a practicing Christian if he believed he was called by God or did he just go and got baptized? He said he was called by God and I responded, "Okay." He asked why did I ask him that question and I again responded, "It is okay." I believed in my heart, if he was called by God, that no matter how far he ran, he would be faced with the reality of his relationship with Jesus.

We were still married when I learned about my first cancer. He was very supportive during that time. It so happened that he was involved in a car accident shortly before I was diagnosed. Thank God he was not hurt too badly and when we learned about my cancer, we saw it as a blessing in disguise. His back was hurt and he had to go to therapy. He was out of work for awhile; he was also free and well enough to take me to my doctor's appointments. My friends were impressed with the attention he was giving to me.

Three years later I was diagnosed with a second cancer. I guess that was too much for him, although he said it was not. It was during this time

THE FACES OF STRUGGLES SUCH AS CANCERS
ARE ON THE JOURNEY TO GOD'S GLORY!

Alfancena Millicent Barrett

he left his job. When I questioned his motive, he said I did not understood why he had to leave his job, he sure did not make me understand. I thought if he had thought hard about his two children and sick wife he would find another job before leaving the one he said he was so disgusted with. He made it worse for me to understand when he played computer games for months instead of looking for a job to take care of his family, especially his children. I had to find ways to provide food for the family. One of my friends helped me get food from a food pantry for six weeks. So for six weeks I had to leave work to go pick up the food.

In spite of all this, I kept trying to let our marriage work; we did marry for better or worse. I also thought it was a phase that would pass. I tired many different ways to add some income to our household. At one point in time, the children and I delivered papers very early in the morning in one of the dangerous part of the city. One of the things I kept to myself, was any of the project where I tried to add income, my husband never showed any interest. If I got him to help with anything, he would do it reluctantly. One of the things I was told before we got married was that he loves his children and that was another plus for me because I love children, too. Living with my husband and seeing how he went about doing things for his children made me say to myself he had a strange way of demonstrating his love for them.

When his son came to live with us, the relationship at first was great. Having a special love for children I was exciting about having his children

THE FACES OF STRUGGLES SUCH AS CANCERS
ARE ON THE JOURNEY TO GOD'S GLORY!

Alfancena Millicent Barrett

sharing in our lives. I had no children of my own so that was even easier for me. The child was home with me most of the time while his dad was at work. I played an active role in his education and development. His son was only eight years old when he came to live with us. Once I took on a parent role in his life, the relationship changed. I did not recognize what was going on at first, but it took me awhile to realize that he was directing the anger he felt towards his mom to me. Over the years we worked through the relationship. One of the things that helped me was some of the teaching I received at bible study. Reading and studying God's words helped me to apply it to my everyday living; as a result, I was able to have a better understanding identifying certain behaviors.

My husband's daughter came to live with us and the relationship was a workable one. She was not happy living with us because she wanted to live with her mom. There was always a back and forth to the mom. She was already a teenager when she came to live with us. The last time she left the house and went to her mom, I told my husband that I cannot keep on doing this. This took place four times and each time we had to make adjustments to accommodate her in our home. After fighting two cancers I did not have it in me to handle that level of stress. I let my husband know that her mother was young and healthy and that was where she wanted to be. I had no problem for him to give his support to his daughter in the environment where she was most comfortable.

He agreed that was best and started out supporting his daughter monetarily. Soon after he started giving his support, he stopped. One of the reasons was, he was not earning enough money and the way he could have more money he did not want to go that route. His daughter's mother was not happy about that and decided to take him to court. As a result of that situation, he wanted his daughter to return to our home so he would not have to pay child support. To this I would not agree. At my refusal he wanted out of the marriage if his daughter could not move back home; I stood my grounds for the fact his daughter was coming to live with us for the wrong reason.

Before the marriage ended, we tried counseling. He went to two sessions out of five, I finished all the other sessions on my own. The second counseling session, the counselor told him that she did not hear me say that I did not want his daughter living within the home, but needed him to consider what I was feeling. He responded that he did not care about my feelings. Those words hit me hard and those words let me know that was the end of the marriage. In the end, he would not communicate with me; and he would not contribute to the expense of the house. He had a child in the house and that did not matter to him. I knew for sure that the Spirit of God was with me throughout that time of my life. We were separated, but in the same house. I experience peace that was only from God. My husband was puzzled by the peacefulness I exercised during that time of turmoil. He reported to one of his cousins about the great relationship his son and I had. That was in spite of his behavior. After everything, the only sad part of the ending of the union was the way it disrupted his son's life, right at the time he was stable and was doing well in school.

In my car I have a container shaped like a loaf of bread with scripture cards that was given to me by a friend during one of my sicknesses. I would read both sides of a card each morning before I drove off to work. One morning while I was getting ready for work I was thinking about the child. When I got to my car, the card I took out to read was very reassuring. It stated "Forasmuch as ye know that your labor is not in vain in the Lord." 1Corinthians 15:58b (KJV). I am happy to report that his son stayed the course and completed high school. There were so many of these verses in morning that gave me strength during that time which I will share at the end of the chapter.

My husband wanted me to move out of the house where I was paying the mortgage. He said he wanted the house for himself to raise his children. According to him, I did not want to be a part of his family anymore. If I had seen any evidence that the place would be taken care of I might have done so. He went as far as to bring a woman in the basement while I was upstairs in my bed. I believed he thought that would really make me leave. I never generally go to the basement unless I was going to do laundry and especially not in the mornings on my way to work. The morning I discovered that scene, I had decided to check on the level of the heating oil because it was late fall and it was cold. It would have been very

THE FACES OF STRUGGLES SUCH AS CANCERS
ARE ON THE JOURNEY TO GOD'S GLORY!

Alfancena Millicent Barrett

dangerous for my health if the oil was gone completely. I was unable to continue automatic delivery because of lack of funds. When I walked down the stairs, I noticed my husband was not alone on his bed, and I thought it was his daughter. I checked to see if it was his daughter and to my surprise it was not; it was a woman. I went upstairs, got my camera, went back down the steps and took a picture. I just thought that no one would believe me if I just tell them. When I took the picture he said it did not matter. The woman was still sleeping, I did not wake her, but at times I wondered what her reaction would have been if I had done so. The interesting thing from that incident, instead of feeling defeated, I felt like I was on top of the world. All I said to God that morning, "You are amazing."

I went to work that morning feeling like I was on cloud nine, my co-workers questioned why I was so happy. I told them what happened and they could not understand my reaction; one of them said to me, "You are something else." I guess when the Spirit of God dwells within you nothing on the outside matters. If I needed confirmation about the ending of that marriage, I sure received it that morning. Apparently, what he did that morning was not enough, he came upstairs fixed breakfast and left the kitchen sink full of dirty dishes. If that was not to drive me out, I don't know what was. I still did not get upset, I just waited until his son came from school and asked him to clean the kitchen up. All I could say about that day, was that I had on the whole armor of God. I later learned that his

THE FACES OF STRUGGLES SUCH AS CANCERS ARE ON THE JOURNEY TO GOD'S GLORY!

Alfancena Millicent Barrett

car broke down that morning.

I thought after getting married at age thirty-eight I would stay married for the rest of my life; I guess it was only a means to an end. My lawyer informed me that whatever assets and liability we had could have been shared evenly or split sixty forty. I was led to draft an agreement concerning our assets and liabilities to which my husband gave his consent. We signed everything in front of a public notary. This was another moment which made me realize that God was with me throughout this ordeal. Who else could have made it possible for such a deal to be struck without any complications? The next event reminded me of the hymn "Each step I take my Savior goes before me..." which was one of my favorites as a young Christian. My husband and his children were on my health insurance plan and it was difficult for me to be paying it without help. I went to my Human Resources office to find out what I could do about it and left there disappointed. I was told he had to move out of the house before he could be removed from my health plan. He did not want to move out until he received his portion of our assets. God demonstrated again that He was in charge of my life, my husband moved out two weeks before open enrollment at my place of work and without his portion of our assets. I was able to renew my health plan just for me. Isn't God truly amazing?

During this time of transition, he did not have a job or a car. He was excited about the prospect of money coming to him. Our assets and liabilities were taken care of before the divorce was finalized. I thank God for the wisdom that He gave me to put everything together and the faith that my husband would agree to everything. I had a lawyer and as a result of what I did, our divorce procedure was not costly. I know, I couldn't have done it without God's help. Our divorce was finalized October, 2006.

My life was so much more peaceful. I did not dream I would be so happy after such an ordeal. It reminded me of when I was a young adult, I often thought about living in the mountains by a stream where I would enjoy God's peace and beauty. I got so much love to give and wanted to love the man I married, but it is very difficult to love someone who does not return the love. Only one person ever did that and that was JESUS. I added divorce to my list of cancers, because during the time I was going through my divorce, I met so many people who were going through separation or a divorce. It was one I survived such like the others.

These are the slices of bread that I fed upon each morning during those difficult days that I would love to share with you. I pray as you read these verses they may speak to you as they did to me.

- *"His compassion fail not They are new every morning."* **Lamentations 3:22b 23a**
- *"God is a refuge for us."* **Psalm 62:8c**
- *"Even the night shall be light about me."* **Psalm 139:11b**
- *"The Lord is nigh unto them that are of a broken heart."* **Psalm 34:18a**
- *"Thou shalt cry and he shall say, Here I am."* **Isaiah 58:9b**

THE FACES OF STRUGGLES SUCH AS CANCERS
ARE ON THE JOURNEY TO GOD'S GLORY!

Alfancena Millicent Barrett

- *"My God shall supply all your need according to his riches in glory."* **Philippians 4:19**
- *"He healeth the broken in heart, and bindeth up their wounds."* **Psalm 147:8**
- *"In returning and rest shall ye be saved."* **Isaiah 30 15b**
- *"The Lord shall give thee rest from thy sorrow."* **Isaiah 14:3a**
- *"I can do all things through Christ which strengtheneth me."* **Philippians 4:13**
- *"The Lord shall give thee rest from thy sorrow."* **Isaiah 14:3a**
- *"I will guide thee with mine eye."* **Psalm 32:8b**
- *"The Lord is thy keeper: the Lord is thy shade upon thy right hand."* **Psalm 121:5**
- *"When thou walkest through the fire, thou shalt not be burned."* **Isaiah 43:2c**
- *"Draw night to God and he will draw night to you."* **James 4:8a**
- *"Through his name whosoever believeth in him shall receive remission of sins."* **Acts 10:43b**
- *"When he hath tried me, I shall come forth as gold."* **Job23:10b**
- *"Forasmuch as ye know that your labor is not in vain in the Lord."* **1Corinthians 15:58b**
- *"Cast thy burden upon the Lord, and he shall sustain."* **Psalm 55:22a**

THE FACES OF STRUGGLES SUCH AS CANCERS
ARE ON THE JOURNEY TO GOD'S GLORY!

Alfancena Millicent Barrett

- *"Commit thy way unto the Lord; trust also in him; and he shall bring it to pass." **Psalm 37:5***
- *"The fear of the Lord tendeth to life: and he that hath it shall abide satisfied." **Proverbs 19: 23ab***
- *"No weapon that is formed against thee shall prosper." **Isaiah 54:17a***
- *"There shall no evil befall thee." **Psalm 91: 10a***
- *"In time of trouble he shall hide me in his pavilion." **Psalm 27:5a***
- *"When thou passeth through the waters, I will be with thee." **Isaiah 43:2a***
- *"They that sow in tears shall reap in joy." **Psalm 126:5***
- *"The Lord shall deliver me from every evil work." **2 Timothy 4:18a***
- *"The angel of the Lord encampeth round about them that fear him, and delivereth them" **Psalm 34:7***
- *"Great peace have they which love thy law." **Psalm 119: 165a***
- *"All things that the Father hath are mine." **John 16:15a***
- *"Many are the afflictions of the righteous: but the Lord delivered him out of them all." **Psalm 34:19***

All scriptures were taken from the King James Version.

THE FACES OF STRUGGLES SUCH AS CANCERS

ARE ON THE JOURNEY TO GOD'S GLORY!

Alfancena Millicent Barrett

CHAPTER 7

MY JOB AS A CLASSROOM LEADER

One day, in the fall 1999, I decided to pay a visit to the college I graduated from early that year to see some of my favorite instructors. I also wanted to "show off" my wedding album because I was still a newlywed. I went to school there for four years and graduated twice with an associate degree in Early Childhood and one in Human Services. So over those four years there were people who were very special to me and some were my friends. When I went in the education department to see one of my instructors, she said she was busy, but asked me to go stop by the Childcare Center which was opened that same fall. She said I was to let the director know that she sent me. The director was very welcoming and gave me a tour of the facility. The tour was very interesting and at the end of the tour the director offered me a job. She told me of the benefits of the job, and I accepted her offer.

I was given the application which I filled out and returned. I was called for an interview shortly after. The process was quick and smooth. I started working January 18th, 2000, as an Infant Classroom Leader. The room was design to accommodate six children. The day I started I had only one student. That worked out well, in the sense that it was my first time working with infants. It gave me a chance to learn a number of things

THE FACES OF STRUGGLES SUCH AS CANCERS
ARE ON THE JOURNEY TO GOD'S GLORY!

Alfancena Millicent Barrett

by the time the room had full capacity. The month of May I had to go to the hospital to do a biopsy on my right lung. This procedure should have taken a few days, but it took weeks for me to be well enough to return to work. It was during that time I learned that I had lymphoma cancer.

When I returned to work everyone was very caring. My co-workers made sure I was doing only what I needed to do and the parents were very encouraging. I was happy I was able to work during treatment. I was glad I was able to continue to nurture the children. Being with those children while going through treatment made the struggle I was going through much easier. The smiles on those faces were the medicine the doctors could not prescribe; working with those young ones was very therapeutic.

I was on a roll in my life free from cancer at least that was what I knew at the time. It was May 2003, this was the year my mother died and this was the year I learned I had breast cancer. They supported me when I lost my mom. When I shared the news of my breast cancer diagnosis with my co-workers some of them were brought to tears. My co-workers and parents came through for me in a big way. It was a bucket of blessings when you worked in a place where you were loved. Most of my co-workers did not call when I was out of work, but I always appreciated the treatment I received whenever I returned.

Since 2005 I had been in and out of the hospital, most of the time for pneumonia. My co-workers handled my absences very well. At times in my absence, my co-workers who worked directly with me got the

THE FACES OF STRUGGLES SUCH AS CANCERS
ARE ON THE JOURNEY TO GOD'S GLORY!

Alfancena Millicent Barrett

opportunity to grow. Sometimes there were struggles to do things the way I did. In the end on my return, they realized that the experiences taught them something new. I was always pleased with the end result. They continued to care about my health and their responsibilities as well.

In 2006 I had to break the news once again to my co-workers that I had cancer, that time it was uterine cancer. I was in my classroom doing my usual thing when one of my co-workers came to me and said that I needed to come talk to a group of co-workers because they were all crying. I responded by questioning why they were crying, and she told me it was because of what I reported to them. I walked in that room and told them that it was going to be alright. After my conversation with them, they left the room smiling. They have never said it to me in so many words, but their behavior told me that they wondered why I was not frightened about facing another cancer.

It was the final week of my recovery from uterine cancer when I learned of my brother's death. My co-workers were very kind and supportive once again. Before the end 2006, I had more bad news to share with my co-workers; I learned that my sister-in-law was diagnosed with cancer and my dad had a stroke. I thanked God to be working with folks like them and the strength He demonstrated through me in their presence. Early in the new year of 2007 they shared with me the passing of my father and my sister-in-law. Through it all, I can say my co-workers and the families of the children I worked with played a huge part in my

THE FACES OF STRUGGLES SUCH AS CANCERS
ARE ON THE JOURNEY TO GOD'S GLORY!

Alfancena Millicent Barrett

healing. There were moments when I shed tears, and it was mainly when I had to leave work because I was not feeling well. A few of my co-workers who witnessed moments like those felt helpless because they often saw me as someone of great strength.

My nine plus years at that job site were great ones. I will never forget and pray I will be well enough to return on a part time basis. I had worked with three directors, cared for many children and parents. I have guided many students and apparently drove fear in some, but many in the end appreciated what I did for them. I have worked and trained many assistances. I had more good times and few conflicts. In the end, my health caused me to leave in the way that was not my desire. I comforted myself in that my life is controlled by God and I have promised to follow His lead. I know the plan God has for my life is perfect. The story of Joseph and Potipher's wife came to me with a new understanding (Genesis 39:7-23KJV) while I was thinking of how I got the job and how I left. God has our life mapped out and sometimes God leads us in directions that we do not choose, but one in which His will be done. When God has an assignment for us, our responsibility is to be humble and listen to his voice.

THE FACES OF STRUGGLES SUCH AS CANCERS
ARE ON THE JOURNEY TO GOD'S GLORY!

Alfancena Millicent Barrett

Contribution from Patricia Williams Former Supervisor and Friend As I Have Known Alfancena Davis

In 1999, I was hired by Delaware Technical and Community College to help create a Child Development Center for the Early Childhood Department (now the Education Department). We opened for the fall semester, but without the Infant Room since I had not found the right Lead Teacher.

One day, Alfancena Davis stopped by the department to share her wedding album with our chair, Dr. Angela Shreve. Angela said that we would be very lucky if we could talk Alfie into taking the position. We asked and she accepted and that began a wonderful professional collaboration and then personal friendship for me with Alfie.

Alfie set to work, making the Infant Room a warm and welcoming place for the babies. She soon had the trust of the parents, the respect of the staff, and the attachment and love of the children. She became famous for the way she could turn the simplest and cheapest materials into wonder creations for the babies to explore. During a week when she was featuring nursery rhymes, I arrived to find some cardboard boxes cut, decorated and laced into a huge shoe with places for the children to crawl and hide. Music and singing from her room spilled into the hallway and office. If I was ever having a hard day, I would go to the rocker in her classroom and feed, read to, or just rock with one of the babies. Alfie's smile and singing would always make me feel better.

THE FACES OF STRUGGLES SUCH AS CANCERS
ARE ON THE JOURNEY TO GOD'S GLORY!

Alfancena Millicent Barrett

It was no wonder that the waiting list for her room grew quickly. I even had a call to put a child on the list and the mother said that I knew about the confirmed pregnancy before the husband. And parents were thrilled whenever they got confirmation that their second child would also get to have Alfie for a teacher.

Another aspect of Alfie's job was to work with the college early childhood students. During their course in Infants and Toddlers, they spent four hours each week working in the Center. Alfie had about 25 students each week and she trained them, supervised them and critiqued their activity plans. As the Center Director, I watched her for several years as she refined this process every semester. Students would begin with fears of handling the babies or being observed or even getting feedback. The good ones always figured out that their time with Alfie was an invaluable part of their education and many transferred their career focus from elementary and preschool level to the infants and toddlers. Later, when I transferred from Director to faculty, I taught the Infants and Toddler course and so I continued with even greater interest as she worked with all of my students.

She also worked with students in their final semester as they did their student teaching experience, working 15 hours each week, eventually taking the role as Lead Teacher for a full week. The other centers in the area quickly caught on that the students from our program were the best, and good infant teachers had their pick of jobs. So Alfie's influence was

THE FACES OF STRUGGLES SUCH AS CANCERS
ARE ON THE JOURNEY TO GOD'S GLORY!
Alfancena Millicent Barrett

spread throughout Wilmington, and even Delaware.

Our Center applied for Accreditation from NAEYC, the National Association for the Education of Young Children and we received it within a year of opening. Alfie was one of three Lead Teachers to help this happen and she worked on the first renewal and then the latest which was much more difficult with higher standards and detailed documentation. The Center also won the Delaware Governor's Award one year and our college honored our Lead Teachers as the team of the year.

It seems that Alfie has struggled all of her life with various health issues. I watched her undergo surgeries, treatments, lose her hair and her physical strength. But her spiritual strength never seemed to wane. She has shown a faith and determination like I have never seen. She even kept on after some of her doctors seemed to have given up. And she found the energy to help others in their fights, too. She began making and selling keepsake pillows to help in the fight against cancer. She made very special pillows for me and my siblings from my mother's fur coat that we all remembered snuggling in church as children.

I have also seen her deal with difficult family issues. There was the illness and death of her parents and siblings in Jamaica where she couldn't be with them as I know she wanted to be. Then she took family members into her home, even adopting a nephew with learning delays. She worked through her own divorce, after years of trying to make the marriage work. I know my own sense of family was strengthened and challenged by her

THE FACES OF STRUGGLES SUCH AS CANCERS
ARE ON THE JOURNEY TO GOD'S GLORY!

Alfancena Millicent Barrett

witness.

She was also there for me when I lost both of my parents, my husband had a serious brain operation and my daughter had surgery. And she celebrated with me on the arrivals of my two grandchildren. It's been an eventful nine plus years.

On the fun and lighter side, I got to share in the excitement as she got her first house and decorated it. She even asked me to make some silk flower arrangements for her. We traded cooking ideas and I learned about many new tastes from Jamaica as she shared her lunches with me. Her curry chicken dish became famous and a "must" at every Center potluck or staff party. I'd spend the whole day looking forward to dinner when I knew it was on the menu. I even kept coming after I moved to faculty.

The last two years have been harder to keep in touch. Alfie's health issues kept her from being at the college. My husband and I moved to Brooklyn and I commuted by train each week, so I was very tired keeping two homes and trying to sell one of them in a bad economy. But when we do talk, it seems like little time has passed and the friendship is still strong as ever. I don't get to Delaware very often now, but seeing Alfie is on the top of my list when I do.

In closing, Alfie has been a wonderful colleague and a good friend. She is one of the most "graceful" people I have ever known. She believes strongly that she is here for a purpose and that the path continually unfolds for her. She is a bringer of blessings and I feel truly blest by knowing her.

CHAPTER 8

CANCER NUMBER ONE – LYMPHOMA

Biopsy

In May of 2000 after a biopsy of my right lung I was diagnosed with non-Hodgkin LYMPHOMA CANCER. Before I was diagnosed I would, at times, burst out into coughing spells and even at times vomit. Once it was over I would feel fine. This would happen at times when I felt hot, cold or got upset. One day I had a strange pain in my back. Whenever the spot was massaged I would give out loud burps. I went to the doctor and I was treated with Pervacid for gas as a result of the signs and symptoms I described. I would still have the coughing episodes, but did not think anything of it. I cannot say for sure how much time elapsed before I was aware of the second pain. I do know it was two days after my wedding. Friends and relatives were teasing me that it was nothing, but all the stuff I was doing with my husband on our wedding night. This was no ordinary pain because this time the pain was accompanied with a temperature.

I went to the doctor and got checked out. The doctor who attended me was not my regular doctor and he said it could be pneumonia. He ordered a chest x-ray for me. I cannot recall if I was called in my doctor's office or I was told over the phone that the result of my chest x-ray was abnormal. I was immediately referred to a pulmonary specialist. He administered a

THE FACES OF STRUGGLES SUCH AS CANCERS
ARE ON THE JOURNEY TO GOD'S GLORY!

Alfancena Millicent Barrett

number of tests none of which discovered what was going on. I got several chest x-ray over the next year, and the abnormality did not decrease or increase. When this all started, my husband and I were living in his cousin's basement with the intention of saving to buy a home. When we learned that something was going on with my lungs, we decided to move just in case something in the basement was contributing to my illness. I did experience a lot of coughing episodes while we were living there.

We found the apartment we were comfortable with and we got settled. The coughing episode ceased, so the doctor waited awhile before doing another x-ray check. There was still no change. All the blood tests and other tests still were unable to identify any problem. The doctor said we have to go inside to see what was going on with my lung. He gave me two options to get this done: a biopsy or a bronchoscopy. I inquired of him which one would give me the best result. He said the biopsy; and I decided to go with that. The doctor told me it was not a difficult procedure and I would be in the hospital for only about two days. Once the decision was made I was referred to the surgeon who gave the same assurance the other doctor gave me. It turned out that I had to beg to leave the hospital on the fourth day. I came home from the hospital with two bags and I was in so much pain I could not sleep in the bed. I remembered my father-in-law had a chair that I thought would work. I had my husband call and he was happy to lend his chair. That chair was my bed for at least a week. To this day I do not believe I was fully healed from that biopsy.

THE FACES OF STRUGGLES SUCH AS CANCERS

ARE ON THE JOURNEY TO GOD'S GLORY!

Alfancena Millicent Barrett

After the biopsy, the surgeon talked with me and told me there was no tumor and at the time that was good news. He also told me the piece of my lung they biopsied was sent off for further testing. A few days later at home I received a call from my doctor's office to come in for an appointment. When I got to my doctor's office, he broke the news to me that I had lymphoma cancer. My doctor told me it was treatable with chemotherapy and if he should have any kind of cancer that would be the one he would want to have. That was reassuring, with that statement I felt I had nothing to fear, and I really did not after leaving my doctor's office. I was referred to the oncologist. I came home, made some calls, and told family and friends the news. In my family, we had no history of cancer. After sharing with them what my doctor said, they were relieved, but said they would all pray.

One day I was at home when I received a call from one of my girlfriends who is like my own sister and a nurse. She said to me, "You know that it is serious," and she explained why. Although I can't remember what she said; that was the first and only time I experienced any moment of tears and sadness. I started to think that I had just started my job and I would not want to lose it. Then the Spirit spoke to me immediately. You are qualified and if you lose that job you can always get another one. After hearing that, my sadness disappeared and never did return throughout my entire ordeal.

THE FACES OF STRUGGLES SUCH AS CANCERS
ARE ON THE JOURNEY TO GOD'S GLORY!

Alfancena Millicent Barrett

Treatment

I am not in the habit of writing a journal, so I do not have exact dates for any of these events. My husband and I met with the oncologist to discuss what was to come and what to expect. Tears did come to my eyes when the doctor said the medications will make me infertile. I was thirty-nine, but was thinking it might still be possible for us to have a child. It did not take long for us to decide it would be fine; my husband was not ready for another child yet and my age was a factor. So there was no need to save any eggs. Another side effect of the medication was that I could lose my hair and I had long, thick hair. I got my hair cut short in preparation of that day. The date for the first treatment was set.

My veins were very small so they had to place a port in my chest to administer the medication. They said my veins would get damaged with the treatment, and I was going to receive twelve rounds of treatment every two weeks. I thank God that He gave me health in an unhealthy situation; and I was able to work during treatment. On treatment days I would go to work, leave half of day, go for treatment, and go home to rest. I would be up and about the next morning for work and would do my hundred percent without any complication.

On the third day of my first treatment, my body started to itch and there were pimples all over my arms, legs and back. I thought it was something I consumed. It was a Friday afternoon and the doctor's office was closed. When I called my oncologist and related what was going on, I

THE FACES OF STRUGGLES SUCH AS CANCERS

ARE ON THE JOURNEY TO GOD'S GLORY!

Alfancena Millicent Barrett

was told to go to the emergency room. The emergency room doctor took a look at me and right away said he did not think it was the chemo medication, it must have been something I ate. I recall that nothing new was eaten except for some grape juice for lunch. It was shortly after that the itching episode started. That was my first diagnosis, but the doctor was so wrong. I had marks on my skin wherever I had itched. I bought a Benadryl cream which helped ease the itching.

My second treatment confirmed that it was the chemo medication which caused the itching. The itching started on the third day after treatment even though they gave me more doses of Benadryl. This time I did not make any new marks on my skin thanks to the Benadryl cream. The palm of my hands, fingers and toe nails turned dark. During that time, I spent a lot of my weekends resting. My right shoulder would hurt especially when I got tired. The fun part was whenever I felt a pain in my shoulders or back and asked to get it massaged, I would get big burps. My co-workers would get a kick out of that.

On my third treatment something went wrong and I did not realize it until the weekend. My left arm was in so much pain. The nurse who administered the medication that trip was not the one who administered my medication the other two times. She must have missed the central area for the medication to go through my vein. I called the doctor's office and told them what was happening. They made immediate arrangements for a mini surgery to remove the port. As a result of that, I was not given

THE FACES OF STRUGGLES SUCH AS CANCERS
ARE ON THE JOURNEY TO GOD'S GLORY!

Alfancena Millicent Barrett

chemotherapy intravenously anymore, but I had to take twelve small tablets every two weeks. I said to one of my sisters who is a nurse, why didn't they give me tablets in the first place. She responded that it was better for me to have gotten it intravenously because it was stronger and worked more effectively.

Receiving treatment for lymphoma had some significant changes in my life. I no longer could eat one of my favorite dishes. I grew up with Jamaican corn beef as part of my diet. Ever since treatment whenever I ate it, I got back pains. After eating it for the third time I realized with the same result it was time to give it up. I thought to myself if that was all I had to give up to stay alive, then it was worth it. I later learned that was not the only thing I had to give up. In Jamaica I grew up with a wide variety of fruits. That was one of the things I missed after leaving Jamaica. Kiwi was one of the fruits I substituted upon coming to the States. It was great going to the farmer's market and getting ten kiwi for a dollar.

One day I came home from work for lunch, I had a sandwich and kiwi as my fruit. As soon as I was finish eating, I brought up everything I had eaten. I did feel better once everything was over. I called work to let them know what had taken place and I was going to take some time to ensure I was okay. After about an hour I returned to work. Earlier that day at work I had hit my head on one of the cupboard doors. When I returned to work my supervisor was almost sure that it had something to do with me getting sick. She had me put ice on the part of my head that I got hit. The security guards came and took a report of the incident. This was how it was confirmed that it was the kiwi. Another day I had lunch at school and the preschoolers had made fruit salad, and I decided to have some. Kiwi was in the salad. I had the same reaction, as soon as I was finish eating the fruit salad; I had to rush to the bathroom. The reaction to the kiwi happened like a flash of lightning and once everything was over I felt fine, just like the last time when I had it. I sure did not try it a third time to confirm my discovery. So I had to say bye-bye to kiwi.

Recovery

The doctors had prescribed nausea medication for me and thank God I did not use it once. I did not lose any of my hair and I felt pretty good most of the time during treatment. The family and friends I had around me made recovery very easy. I received cards that were inspirational and encouraging. The cards I still do have and still read at times. One day I plan to recycle them not because they are old cards, but to share the joy I received during those difficult times. My name was on so many prayer list here in the United States, Canada and Jamaica. God must have questioned what is it about this person that I needed to keep her alive. I do not believe it was because I was special, but God knew my imperfection and planned to help me reach that point of holiness. At the end of my treatment I was grateful to God that I was given a second chance to life. Each day I live to the fullest, knowing God has kept me for His purpose.

THE FACES OF STRUGGLES SUCH AS CANCERS
ARE ON THE JOURNEY TO GOD'S GLORY!

Alfancena Millicent Barrett

At the end of my final treatment, my marching orders were that I had to check with my oncologist every six months. My family doctor was very knowledgeable, in my opinion, and was also very honest about my prognosis. He told me because of the lymphoma, I am ten percent likely to get another cancer and that risk was too high. As a result of that, I really learned about my body and pay attention to unusual signs or symptoms. I visit my doctor as soon as anything is out of whack. My doctor always administers the necessary test to rule everything out. I also make sure I have all my yearly routine examinations.

CHAPTER 9

CANCER NUMBER TWO - BREAST CANCER

I had my yearly mammogram done in April 2003. This was the first time since I had been getting my mammogram three years ago that I was called back to repeat the test. I did not only repeat the test, but I had an ultra sound done, too. At the end of the test, I was taken to see the doctor. In my mind this was serious, but I was not frightened. The doctor told me it appeared to be a cyst and it was nothing to worry about; but we will keep a check on it. I left the doctor's office relieved.

Sometime in June I came home from work and lay on a cot in my home office for a nap. I woke up from my nap with a sharp and strange pain in my right breast. I called my doctor's office the next day and scheduled an appointment. Shortly after that pain and before my appointment, I felt a mass on the side of my right breast. The day of my appointment my doctor confirmed that something was different with my right breast when he compared it with my left. He said he needed me to go see a breast specialist, and I was given the number by his staff. I called the specialist's office and the earliest date I could get an appointment was July seventeenth, 2003. In my mind that appointment was too far off, but I had no choice because I was a new patient. I had to cancel that appointment because my mom went home to glory on July sixth, 2003. I had to leave for Jamaica for mom's "Home Going".

Wow, with the sadness of my mother's passing and concern about the mass on my right breast, I was not depressed. That had to be the Spirit of God that surrounded me. I spent my time and effort ensuring that my mom had a wonderful "Home Going". During this, my family members and relatives talked about my strength; but that was the power of God they were seeing in me. We talked about what was going on with my breast, and we prayed that it would be nothing.

Biopsy

I returned to the United States near the end of July after my mom's funeral. I called and rescheduled my appointment with the breast doctor. I am not good with dates, but I am good at telling the sequence of events. The appointment date finally came. The staff at the breast doctor's office was very pleasant, and I felt very relaxed as a result. The doctor appeared to specialize in ensuring that her patients had nothing to worry about, that was how I felt when she had finished talking with me. I had a fine needle aspiration done and my doctor was hoping it was the lymphoma returned and not breast cancer. The lymphoma I had was more treatable than breast cancer.

A few days later after that procedure I received a call from the doctor's office. I had to go in for another test. The doctor reported that there was a sign of cancer in the specimen they had gotten the first time, but it was not

THE FACES OF STRUGGLES SUCH AS CANCERS
ARE ON THE JOURNEY TO GOD'S GLORY!

Alfancena Millicent Barrett

enough to determine what kind of cancer it was. This time I had to do a big needle aspiration and that was painful. A few days later after that test, I learned my fate. The findings were that I had breast cancer, lobular invasive carcinoma. It was a stage one and surgery was immediately scheduled for the following week. I had to have a full mastectomy on my right breast. The doctor said the mass spread over a wide area and that would be the best way to ensure getting all the bad cells. I did notice a lot more attention was given to the breast cancer than the lymphoma.

I met with a medical team this time, which included other doctors, a nurse and a social worker. I did not use any of the services offered by the medical team. I guess after listening to me, they must have said among themselves she does not need any of our services. I was not depressed or in despair about my situation. I also met with the plastic surgeon to discuss the options of replacing my breast after surgery. For me it was another chapter in my life that God was going to take me through.

Surgery

It was a Friday in August of 2003 and the day for my surgery. The day I was going to lose my right breast. My husband took me to the hospital, but had to leave for work. I did not have my mother or my sister to be with me, but God provided two of my church sisters who stayed with me all day. They were with me before I went off to surgery and were there when I woke up from surgery. During situations like that made me understand

THE FACES OF STRUGGLES SUCH AS CANCERS
ARE ON THE JOURNEY TO GOD'S GLORY!

Alfancena Millicent Barrett

these words even more -"*God will not lead you, where He will not provide for you.*" God provided family when I needed them.

The operating room was buzzing when I entered. There was a team of people around me, each member telling me his or her name and the purpose of his or her presence. They were very pleasant too, and I felt very comfortable. Once I received the sleeping medication I was out before they finished administering it. The next thing I was aware of someone waking me up in the recovery room. The doctor told me everything went well with the surgery; and they only took a few lymph nodes because the ones they took out were negative. That was a bit of good news.

I spent a few days in the hospital before I went home with my two drainage bags. I had one severe pain the night after surgery and that was the last time I had pain during the recovery period. When friends came by to visit me the day after surgery they could not believe it. I was moving around as if I had surgery a few days ago.

In a week after surgery I was seen by one of the surgeon's associates, because she went on vacation. The doctor said everything looked good. A week later which would be two weeks after surgery, I saw the surgeon. She was amazed at how fast I healed. Isn't God amazing? She advised me to stay home two more weeks before returning to work. She also wrote a prescription for me to get a prosthesis. I left the doctor's office very excited and went right to the store to pick up my new prosthetic breast.

This store had all kinds of items for cancer patients especially breast

THE FACES OF STRUGGLES SUCH AS CANCERS
ARE ON THE JOURNEY TO GOD'S GLORY!

Alfancena Millicent Barrett

cancer. I told the clerk the purpose of my visit and handed her the prescription. She asked me how long ago I had surgery. I told her two weeks ago and her response was that I would not be ready for a prosthesis. She went on to say it takes about four weeks to be healed from such a surgery. She said she would take a look anyway. When she saw my scar, she was in disbelief; she could not believe I was really healed. She was so impressed; she gave me a donated one since I was planning to reconstruct my breast. I walked out of that store with my new breast. I returned to work two weeks later as the doctor ordered. It was good to be back at work.

I still wear a prosthesis today. I tried the tram flap reconstruction for my right breast, but it did not take. I had surgery one week for the reconstruction and then had to have another surgery to take it off the following week before I developed an infection. When I left work to get this procedure done, I told my co-workers and families that I would be back with new "boobs" and flat tummy. You see, the doctor was going to reconstruct my right breast, reduce my left so my breast would be like when I was a young adult. You can image how disappointing that was for me when I was unable to show off the new me. As a result I was away from work for nine weeks instead of six. The plastic surgeon said that we could try again, but I decided against it. My husband at the time said he was fine with my one breast, but looking back I think he was lying. I told

THE FACES OF STRUGGLES SUCH AS CANCERS
ARE ON THE JOURNEY TO GOD'S GLORY!

Alfancena Millicent Barrett

the doctor my life does not depend upon this surgery so there was no need to try again.

Treatment

I met with my oncologist and discussed treatment. I was going to get three rounds of chemo therapy every three weeks. Radiation would follow chemo for about five weeks. Chemo went well, but between my first and second treatment I lost my hair. I came home from church one Sunday place my fingers in my hair and when I removed my fingers I realized my hair was coming out. Most of my hair came out with my fingers. I called my father-in-law and asked him to come over to cut the rest off. Later that day my head was all bald. Every one told me I had a great shape head and I looked like an African model. I had a great time wearing my bald head. I would only wear a hat when I went to church. I believed that would be a distraction and church was not the place for that, it is a place of worship. When my hair started to fall out, I remembered my visit from a lovely lady from the Cancer Society. She was a breast cancer survivor herself and she told me she did not lose her hair until she got sick and took the antibiotic. I wondered if that was why I lost my hair this time around with chemo.

I developed strep throat after my first treatment and had to be given an antibiotic; with the antibiotic I developed a yeast infection and it was the next day after taking fluconazole that I started to lose my hair. So I cannot say for sure if it was just the chemo that caused me to lose my hair, especially since I did not lose it the first time I took chemo. My hair grew back soon after chemo, softer and curlier. I was hoping it would not grow back as thick as it was, but it did. I found it amusing when I went to church without hat soon after my hair started to grow. Everyone was crazy about my hair and how it looked so good. One sister said to me, "I do not know why you cut your hair, but boy it sure looks good." I just smiled and said, "Thank you," and I did not tell her the real reason why. My friend from the Cancer Society also gave me a small pillow which I still have today. She demonstrated how I could use the pillow for comfort while I was healing from surgery.

Radiation

Soon after chemo I had my appointment with the Radiation Oncologist. The staff at this facility was very warm and I felt I knew them from way back when. In my opinion they were very professional. I went for radiation treatment every morning before going to work, Monday through Friday for about five weeks. I was always grateful to God that each morning He gave me health in an unhealthy body. I was able to go to work and perform a full day's work as if everything was normal. At the end of the working day I would take a nap before trying to do any chores at home.

At the end of radiation, I was presented with a certificate for the completion of my radiation treatment. I thought that was so cool. A few

THE FACES OF STRUGGLES SUCH AS CANCERS
ARE ON THE JOURNEY TO GOD'S GLORY!

Alfancena Millicent Barrett

days after radiation treatment the area got so sore I could not wear the prosthesis for about two weeks. I would wear big tops so it was not so obvious when I walked around. Family members and friends knew the real deal. When I was able to wear my prosthesis again, I started to have aches in my back. It was so painful that I told my family doctor. He asked me if the prosthesis was heavy and I said, "Yes." He told me the back pain was from the prosthesis and I should make sure my bra straps were adjusted properly. Believe me, there was a difference. So when I went to get my new prosthesis I was happy to learn that they had them in light weight. I was a little disheartened when my co-pay was higher, but getting the light boob was worth every penny.

One fun part of the treatment was going to physical therapy. I had to go to therapy to stretch my arm on the side I had the mastectomy. My arm could hardly raise above my head after healing from surgery and I also needed to learn how to prevent lymphedema. My therapist appeared to be a very caring individual and she was very patient. At first the exercises looked a little silly, but were not easy to do, but they were very effective. I had one of the exercises where I had to walk my fingers up a wall; with that exercise I was able to use my right arm a lot more.

What Breast Cancer Did For Me

One day I received a letter from the Delaware Breast Cancer Coalition (DBCC) inviting me to be a member of the Young Survivors. I am sure

THE FACES OF STRUGGLES SUCH AS CANCERS
ARE ON THE JOURNEY TO GOD'S GLORY!

Alfancena Millicent Barrett

glad I did because being a member gave me a lot of pleasant experiences. As a member of the group, I was given the opportunity to volunteer and attend special events. Some of the events were "Tea Party" at the Goodstay Mansion, "Wings of Hope" at the Waterfall Banquet Hall, and the Delaware Breast Cancer Coalition annual fundraising event. The best part of the fundraising was that I got to be a model. Why was that so much fun? I got to go to the beauty salon, where I could not afford to get my hair and face done. I also got to walk around all afternoon in clothes that I couldn't afford not even at discounted price. It was so good to get dressed-up at somebody else's expense.

One year I got the opportunity to rub shoulders with some of Delaware's rich and famous, doctors and other medical professional. I was eating unusual finger snacks and sipping red wine. I was featured in the Delaware Breast Cancer Coalition magazine and on the home page website. One year I was asked to give a presentation at the fundraiser titled "What the Delaware Breast Cancer Coalition Meant to Me." When I volunteered at certain events, I got the opportunity to share my story. I was able to encourage other women to get their yearly mammogram, learn about their bodies and to practice self examination.

I participated in one event as a young survivor that I will never forget; it was one where I gained some friends, ones I still have today. My most memorable event was being featured in the News Journal, Delaware's number one newspaper. Even today, if you Google my name, you can still

THE FACES OF STRUGGLES SUCH AS CANCERS
ARE ON THE JOURNEY TO GOD'S GLORY!

Alfancena Millicent Barrett

find it and that was one of the reasons it was so unforgettable. During the summer of 2005 I attended an art program at the Delaware Center for the Contemporary Arts under the leadership of a sculptor from Erie, Pennsylvania; in the company of eleven beautiful women. That was when it came to me that being a survivor was not so bad after all. I also realized that cancer did not come to destroy me, but to take me places. I got to do some interesting things and I learned how to carve a picture in linoleum.

I had to write a piece associated with my art work to compile a book with the other ladies art work. This was what I wrote- "*I AM A SURVIVOR*: As a survivor, I have come to realize that cancer does not always come to destroy you, but to take you places. Since my cancers, I have met some wonderful people in my life. One of the paths led me to share in an art class of expressive women and a lovely art teacher; the way we bonded in spite of our differences was amazing. This class brought out an artistic touch which was buried deep within. My art piece represents the strength I had after recovering from complications even after the cancers went into remission. My print name was *THE GARDEN OF STRENGTH.*"

The pages in my book will remind me of each face and what each individual had been through and how strong they were. I saw this as just another chapter in my life. On my journey of life I have a lot more places to go and see."

This was what my art teacher wrote about me -

Dear Alfie, Your boundless creativity and radiant smile have brought

THE FACES OF STRUGGLES SUCH AS CANCERS
ARE ON THE JOURNEY TO GOD'S GLORY!

Alfancena Millicent Barrett

so much to the class. Don't stop creating; your young students are so lucky!" Suzanne

Being married and having financial problems caused great strain on my household. Thinking how I could change things, I remembered those words of the art instructor. I decided to use my creativity and make pillows to sell. I discussed it with my husband and he sounded like he was excited. He mentioned building a website to advertise. I got started making the pillows. I planned to tithe; donate a percentage to the Delaware Breast Cancer Coalition; The Cancer Society and Sisters On A Mission. One day while preparing the pillows a light bulb came on that I should have a pillow party and have talks on early detection.

I took pictures of each pillow I made because each one needed to be special. I called them "Keepsake Pillows." I wanted them to be for someone who is a survivor, know someone who is a survivor or in memory of someone who passed away as a result of cancer. The pillows were often made with a pocket to place keepsake items in it, even a picture. The first party was at my house and it was a huge success. My husband used the pictures I took of the pillows, and made a slide show. I really appreciated that because it enhanced the party. Twenty-two ladies attended, and they were impressed with the information they received. One of my friends from the Delaware Breast Cancer Coalition gave the talk, she was very effective. I believe she was born and became a survivor, just for that purpose. The ladies were excited about the pillows, too. It was

THE FACES OF STRUGGLES SUCH AS CANCERS
ARE ON THE JOURNEY TO GOD'S GLORY!

Alfancena Millicent Barrett

shortly after the party that my husband and I started to drift in different directions. Our relationship soon ended in divorce. I did not get the website I was dreaming of nor the business. I had a few more house parties that were all a success in terms of women getting information; some of the parties were not successful financially. I got sick again which prevented me from going forward, but I have hope that one day I will be well enough to start again spreading the word about early detection. Early detection does save lives.

When I was thinking of another chapter in my life, I was not thinking that I was going to journey through another cancer, but I did. Whenever I went for an x-ray I often thought of my childhood, thinking that none of the machines looked familiar. Back then I was stripped of my clothing and placed on a cold metal table with a strange apparatus above me. It did finally happen one day; I walked in the room and there was an x-ray table that reminded me of those days. The flood gates of my eyes opened, but was not for my present circumstances; it was the fact that God had brought me to this point of my life amid all that I been through.

CHAPTER 10

CANCER NUMBER THREE – UTERINE

Diagnosis

When my doctor told me I would likely get another cancer I did not think I would have two others. I was in remission from breast cancer, but was in and out of the hospital for pneumonia and pleurisy. Just at the time when I was feeling great and I was thinking I am out of the woods; I was hit with the news of another cancer. During this time I was also faced with the cancer of divorce. I thought it was the lymphoma cancer returning, but no, it was a new cancer. I was taking Tamoxifen to prevent the return of breast cancer. One of the side effects for Tamoxifen is uterine cancer and sure enough I got uterine cancer. I did notice a pattern, I was getting attacked by a cancer every three years, lymphoma 2000; breast 2003; uterine 2006; lymphoma showed up in 2008, but the treatment I received apparently did not take care of it, so it showed up more forcefully in 2009. Also, it appeared the cancers came with a companion, the year I was diagnosed with breast cancer my mother died; the year I was diagnosed with uterine cancer my brother died.

Treatment for breast cancer sent me into early menopause. I had no complaints because I did not have to worry about that monthly ordeal. I started to spot two years later, but did not think anything was serious.

THE FACES OF STRUGGLES SUCH AS CANCERS
ARE ON THE JOURNEY TO GOD'S GLORY!

Alfancena Millicent Barrett

There was the possibility my period would return. I went to the doctor just to ensure that the spotting was not from any other underlying problem. My doctor sent me to do an ultra sound in order to rule anything out as he always did. That night after the ultra sound I bled until I was weak. I had to call out from work. I called my doctor's office the next morning, and he advised me to go see my gynecologist. During this time my husband and I were separated, I was upstairs and he was downstairs in the basement. He was not aware of what was going on with me.

I went to the appointment and my gynecologist performed biopsy on my uterus. I had to go back to the gynecologist to get another one done because the first sample had too much blood and was unable to detect any problem. A few days after the second procedure I was summoned to the doctor's office. The doctor reported to me that it was uterine cancer, but it was in the early stage. We discussed a treatment plan. I was going to have a complete hysterectomy. I was going to lose my ovaries, fallopian tubes and uterus. At that time after hearing this, I said to myself. "God is truly amazing; they can take parts of my body and I keep on living." Surgery was scheduled for May eighteen, 2006, the same day as my job's recognition day ceremony which was mandatory. Getting my surgery done superseded any recognition ceremony. I had to write a letter to the proper authorities to be excused.

I also realized not only did the cancer occur every three years, but I got diagnosed in the same month May. As I mentioned before, my husband was not aware of what was going on with me and since he was leaving, there was no need to tell him. My husband left our home during this time. He and his children were on my health insurance, and I was unable to take them off unless we had different addresses. He moved out two weeks before open enrollment. I was able to renew for my insurance with just me...amazing!

We had an agreement in which I would give him money towards his portion of our assets. I had to get the house refinanced in order to get the money. He had to go to the closing in order to sign his name off the deed. My surgery was scheduled for May eighteen and the closing for May sixteen. I was happy that I was able to take care of this settlement before surgery. We had to go some distance away from home, so we made arrangements to meet at the bank's lawyer's office. He had to arrange a ride to go because his car was stolen. The day before the appointment he called me and said he did not have a ride and could he have a ride with me. At that point I had no choice; I needed to get this behind me. We rode together that long distance and thank God we were able to have a pleasant conversation.

Surgery

I reported to the outpatient department on the day of surgery. I was prepped soon after my arrival for surgery. My gynecologist/surgeon came and talked with me before they put me to sleep. He reminded me of what we were about to do and that there would be another specialist who was going to be present in the operating room. His purpose was to be on standby in case the lymph nodes from my groin were positive. Thanks be to God they were not. Surgery went well, and I did not have a lot of pain. My brother called me from out of state the day after surgery and when I answered the phone he was in disbelief. He said that I did not sound like someone who just had a major surgery. I went home in a couple of days to start recovery, but God already started the healing process as soon as the surgery was over.

Recovery

I was coming home from the hospital to an empty house, but here was another instance how God showed me how much He loved and care about me. God provided caretakers for me in a way I did not dream of for the first three weeks of my recovery. People who I just became friends with, and friends who I have not seen or communicated with in awhile, were all willing to assist in my recovery. Guess who was upset and hurt that I did not tell him I was having surgery? Yes, my ex-husband. My response to him was; you were the one who said you did not care about my feelings to my face in the presence of the counselor. The way I felt, he did not only say those words, but his action also showed it. I thought to myself that he might be regretting that he left the house already because if I am plagued with another cancer I might not be around very long.

THE FACES OF STRUGGLES SUCH AS CANCERS
ARE ON THE JOURNEY TO GOD'S GLORY!

Alfancena Millicent Barrett

His behavior confirmed my thoughts a few days later. The check we received from the refinancing had to take a few days to be cleared from the bank. My ex-husband called on the very day the check was scheduled to be ready. However, that day was only three days after coming home from the hospital. I was barely going up and down the stairs. I mentioned that to him and the fact that he agreed to clean the basement before the money was handed over to him. He got very upset when I said that and let me know in no uncertain terms that I was holding up his life. That was the last thing I would want to do. So I called my job and asked one of my co-workers for a ride to the bank, I could barely walk, but I made it. I gave him his money so he could move on with his life. I was happy that I could do that for him.

The second to last week of my recovery period I got a call from Jamaica that my brother was rushed to the hospital. Before the night was over he was gone. I had to make plans to go to Jamaica to bury my brother. One of my dear cousins did not hesitate to take care of my plane fare. When she ordered my ticket, she also ordered wheelchair assistance. That really helped because I was not totally healed. I remembered many at the airport had a certain look in their eyes as if to say, "She doesn't look like she needs a wheelchair." God's grace and mercy helped me to make it through that valley of my life. Healing took place in spite of all the struggles. I came to learn that trials only come our way to make us

THE FACES OF STRUGGLES SUCH AS CANCERS
ARE ON THE JOURNEY TO GOD'S GLORY!

Alfancena Millicent Barrett

stronger. The uterine cancer was the easiest to be treated, but I went through some serious tests during that time.

THE FACES OF STRUGGLES SUCH AS CANCERS
ARE ON THE JOURNEY TO GOD'S GLORY!

Alfancena Millicent Barrett

CHAPTER 11

A SPECIAL ASSIGNMENT I RECEIVED FROM GOD

My brother Villair had a great "Home Going" and like many funerals around the world. Although it is a time of sadness, it is always a time for reunions. You are reunited with folks from primary school, high school, college and from anywhere else that you have met and known them in your life time. I returned to the United States feeling greatly rejuvenated from my experiences. Approximately two months after my brother's funeral I got a call from my niece and sister-in-law. After the greetings, the conversation started out like this; "You are the first to know that I was diagnosed with gall bladder cancer." I was stunned because I just left a healthy woman in Jamaica, as far as the human eyes could see. The treatment plan they described to me appeared to be simple. She was going to have surgery to remove the gall bladder. The conversation ended with us committing it all in God's hands.

The day of my sister-in-law's surgery we prayed that it would be successful. I later received a call that they were unable to take out the gall bladder because the cancer had spread to other organs. That was the kind of news no one wanted to hear. I was happy after all that my sister-in-law was in good spirit. She did not accept the answer the doctors gave her. She was prepared to fight and seek other opinions. She was blessed that she had a visa to travel to the United States to get checked out. It was very sad when she checked out the other sources and received the same answer. She still did not give in to despair; she said it was all in God's hands. In less than a year after the diagnosis and the death of my brother, God chose to take her home. Healing for her was not on this side of Heaven, but on the other side.

She had three children, two grown and the other only eleven years old. The eleven year old is a functioning Down Syndrome child. The environment where he was did not cater to his needs, and I was led to be the one to be responsible for him. He had no parents, and I felt that was one of the reasons God kept me alive. I had all the resources to cater to his needs and I know he would get the love and attention he needed. My divorce was final and I was free and single again. I was free to pursue any adventure or a relationship if I chose to, but the well being of my nephew meant the world to me. As a result of my decision, I prayed a prayer and I got an instant answer. It was unbelievable. I said to God, you create emotions and you know my desire is to serve you, so please put my emotions in check. God did that for me and today although I am alone (not in a relationship) I have never been lonely. I also got a better understanding of **Philippians 4:19 (KJV) "But my God shall supply all your needs according to his riches in glory by Christ Jesus."** He promised to supply our needs not our wants; therefore anything I desire and did not get, it was not a need. Once I understood that clearly my focus

THE FACES OF STRUGGLES SUCH AS CANCERS
ARE ON THE JOURNEY TO GOD'S GLORY!

Alfancena Millicent Barrett

was on my nephew.

I had to get him settled in his new environment and to make him legally my son. He came to me shortly after his mother was laid to rest. I did not know how things were going to go because I had no idea how to go about getting the adoption done. My faith in God gave me the assurance that all would be well. Every day Jesus helped me to understand even more that when God is in the plan, He opens doors you had no idea would open. One day at work I saw one of my past parent who happened to come by, and I was very happy to see her. I shared with her my story about my nephew and sure enough she was able to give me a contact person who would be able to answer my questions. She was a very resourceful individual who I knew had done adoptions in the pass and who I believed was sent by God that day.

I contacted the individual she recommended and received some useful information. My first step in the process was to get guardianship of my nephew and this had to be done through the family court. I was not yet a citizen and I was excited when I learned that I did not have to be a citizen in the State of Delaware to file an adoption. He had to be in my guardianship for a year before I could file for the adoption. It was amazing that each question I had about the situation God placed someone in my path to provide the answer. He got registered in school. Each step I took to get him settled in his new environment was easier than the first. He was also welcomed warmly by my church family and that made me very

THE FACES OF STRUGGLES SUCH AS CANCERS
ARE ON THE JOURNEY TO GOD'S GLORY!

Alfancena Millicent Barrett

happy.

By the end of the summer he was more comfortable with his new environment. He did not handle the changes very well at first and it took me awhile to realize that the behavior he was displaying was a result of him not being able to express his feelings. His receptive language was great, but his expressive language was weak. He is a lovely child. He keeps his room clean and neat. He likes to see everything in place. He is very helpful; he does not just take the groceries from the car, he unpacks them without being told to do so. At times he opens my car door and allows me to get in or out. He is also safety conscious, as soon as he would get into a car; he puts his seatbelt on. If I did not put mine on right away, he would let me know I that should put my seatbelt on. One could not ask to take care of a better child than that.

A home study was a part of the adoption process. It was great that I was able to get the home study done while I was waiting for the year to end to file the adoption with the court. The case worker for the home study was a very sweet individual. The adoption agency I was working with closed shortly after the home study was completed. I felt very blessed that I did not have to seek help elsewhere. They told me they did all they could for me, and I just needed a family lawyer to complete the process. The lawyer I had originally consulted no longer worked for that company, so I had to seek another attorney. I remembered that one of my church sisters was a lawyer. I called her and she was very excited to assist me; she said

THE FACES OF STRUGGLES SUCH AS CANCERS
ARE ON THE JOURNEY TO GOD'S GLORY!

Alfancena Millicent Barrett

she did know a family lawyer and she had seen her only yesterday. She gave me the information to get in touch with the lawyer.

I got in touch with the lawyer and set up the appointment. We met and she went over the details. Soon after I retained her, in no time the adoption was final. I had all the documents that were required so there was no need for a court hearing. He was now officially my son. I still had one more hurdle to go over, his immigration status had to be changed. He had to live with me physically for two years before I could even start that process. It was another hurdle God was going to help me cross. While I was waiting to have his status changed, I changed my status from a resident to a citizen of the United States. Six months after my application I was sworn in as a United States citizen. That was a proud moment. I had fun studying for the civics test, I had my co-workers helping me and in return they were learning about their country.

The year 2007 was a very healthy one for me. I only went to the doctors for annual check-ups and I was able to pass the physical to ensure that I was fit enough to be an adoptive parent. Starting in 2008, I started having health issues and had to be in the hospital at times. Let me mention how God's plan is always perfect; my adoptive son's brother found a job in the Delaware valley. What was even more amazing he bought a house on the next street over and if it was not for the house on the corner of my street, I could stay at my front door and see his front door. The house was on the market for only four days and he won the bid over four other families. So each time I had to go to the hospital, my son stayed with his brother and family. That had to be a part of God's divine plan; he was with family and he was not far from home.

He affectionately called me Auntie Millie and I did not explain the whole adoption to him, because I did not think he would understand. During his first year here, whenever someone called from Jamaica he would ask them about his Mom and Dad. One night I heard him say "Goodnight mom," this happened two weeks before Mother's Day 2009. I was really touched by those words. At that point I believe I am going to be physically well in order to help this child prepare for the purpose God has planned for him. He loves cars, especially matchbox ones. Music is a big part of his world too. He uses the back of the church bench as his keyboard every Sunday when he goes to church. He received two key board from folks at church as a result; one electrically operated and the other operated by battery. I have high hopes that he will be able play a tune one day.

His love for cars had me thinking how I would get him in the field to learn more about them and for him to work with real cars later. His teacher in middle school thought he could learn how to do car detailing and believed that he would be good at it. I believe he will eventually attend a vocational school to develop that skill. He was very popular especially with the girls at his middle school. His teacher reported that he was very respectful and helpful. He loves art and was very good at cleaning up his work area. He is a very observant child; he is able to repeat many actions he observed. I do not leave my car keys careless because he observes everything that I do whenever we get in the car. One afternoon we came home after work and school and he put the car in park as soon as I stopped the car. I had to discourage his assistance on that assignment because of my fears that he would try to drive the car. He has a very good sense of direction; he only has to go somewhere once and he can return to that area independently.

This child makes life so interesting and I believe he is one of the reasons God kept me after so many struggles with my health. God needed me to prepare him for something greater. I pray daily that I will carry out this task with humility.

CHAPTER 12

REVISIT FROM NUMBER ONE CANCER - LYMPHOMA

Since 2005 I have gone so many times to the hospital that I stop counting. After so many visits I started telling my friends and family that I am spending time at the hotel. I told them I could not afford this "vacation" elsewhere; I have the comfort of the hospital room; room service for my meals; and other needs being met just by pressing a button! Those moments oftentimes gave me the opportunity to be still and witness the most beautiful sceneries of God's creation. On one of my visits there was one of the views that fascinated me the most and also reminded me of home that I will share. I saw the Brandywine River flowing through the trees. I saw the Delaware River and a boat going by. I saw birds flying, vehicles going by and people walking. I saw beautiful cloud formation hanging in the bright blue sky. The best part of that scenery was the big cobweb on the outside of my window. My diagnosis was oftentimes pneumonia and a few times pleurisy on my visits.

In the summer of 2008 on one of my hospital visits; I was attended by a new and young pulmonary specialist. He stated in our discussion that with my history of cancer we need to check out why I was having pneumonia so often. A bronchoscopy was scheduled while I was in the hospital. The result of the procedure came back that there were signs of

THE FACES OF STRUGGLES SUCH AS CANCERS
ARE ON THE JOURNEY TO GOD'S GLORY!

Alfancena Millicent Barrett

lymphoma in my lungs. My oncologist first treated me with Prevpac because he said that bacteria could have caused the lymphoma to show up. One of sisters, who is a nurse, did not like that; I guess she was right, because that medication did not help. I had to be treated with a chemo medication. I was given Rituximab only and was feeling good after the treatment. I had to visit the hospital during this time because I believe I had a bad reaction when the Rituximab and Floradil, a medication for asthma mixed. Looking back now, in my opinion, all those times I was treated for asthma, it was the lymphoma in my body that was the culprit and not asthma. Three months after treatment I went for a checkup and I was given an okay from the doctor. My next visit would be in six months. When I left the doctor's office I remembered that I had mentioned to him about a pain in my stomach, but he did not address it.

The pain was not a constant pain, it surfaced every now and then, I forgot about it most time. I did not bother to contact the doctor once I got home. December 2008, I went to the hospital for pneumonia. In January of 2009 the pain in my stomach resurfaced; it would do so once or twice a week. I decided to go see my family doctor about the pain before it got worse. When I got to my doctor's office, he listened to my chest, he said I was wheezing and asked the nurse to administer a treatment. He said he was treating me so I wouldn't have to end up in the hospital. I was treated for the wheezing and was given medication for the stomach. When I got home, I took the medication for my stomach, and then had dinner. That

THE FACES OF STRUGGLES SUCH AS CANCERS
ARE ON THE JOURNEY TO GOD'S GLORY!

Alfancena Millicent Barrett

night I had the worst pain of my life in my belly. I was not blessed to bear children, but could only imagine it was the kind of pain mothers bore when having children. I could not sit, I could not lie down and I could barely walk. I went downstairs and made a cup of tea thinking that would help. I had a few burps but the pain continued. I went to the bathroom and gas came out like an explosion, but the pain did not go away. It was almost morning when the pain finally calmed down and I was able to rest. I called out from work and went back to the doctor. My regular doctor was not there; and I really don't like seeing other doctors, but I had no choice. When the doctor saw me, she told me to head to the emergency room, I was still in pain.

They kept me in the hospital. I was worried about my stomach, they did the CAT scan; they saw nothing wrong with my stomach, but pneumonia was present. So attention was given to my lungs and not my stomach. I asked about the pain in my stomach, but there was no explanation. The medication I received in the hospital eased the pain. I told my doctor when he visited me that I need my stomach checked out. He said we will get it done as an outpatient procedure because it was the weekend and nothing would be done until Monday. I got discharged from the hospital. I called and scheduled the appointment for an endoscopy. I learned on the same day that my stomach was all sore and a specimen was sent off for further testing. I went back for post endoscopy and the doctor reported that there were abnormal 'A' typical lymphocytes; he was still waiting for result of further testing. I asked for a copy of the report and took it to my family doctor.

When my doctor read the report, he said the lymphoma was back and he had that concern when he saw my last chest x-ray while I was in the hospital in December 2008. My doctor said I would need to be treated again with chemotherapy. I came home, called and made an appointment with my oncologist. My oncologist looked at the report from the doctor, typed a bunch a stuff on his laptop while he was talking to me; but he really didn't look at me. He examined me. He said I should repeat the test in four months. I asked him if he was not going to treat me; he responded that there was nothing to treat because the report just said it was an 'A' typical cell and did not specify lymphoma. I guess his way of assuring me was to let me know he would check with the pathologist for the result of the further testing. I left the doctor's office not satisfy. I am not a medical personnel, but I could not understand why the doctor took it so lightly when the result talked about lymphocytes cells. I have a history of lymphoma and my body was still not feeling right. *I have learned one of the keys to discovering cancer was that I knew my body well enough to know when something was wrong.*

I waited a few days before calling the oncologist's office. When I called he responded that the pathologist confirmed that it was the same thing that was in my lungs that was in my stomach. He did not use the word lymphoma. He told me over the phone that he was going to have me

THE FACES OF STRUGGLES SUCH AS CANCERS
ARE ON THE JOURNEY TO GOD'S GLORY!

Alfancena Millicent Barrett

do a PET scan. I can't recall if he was the one who gave me the appointment time and date or his office staff. The day of the PET scan I had a temperature and I heard my chest wheezing. Thank God, that the way I was feeling did not stop the test. I went home to wait for the result. I had called out from work for a few days. I called my pulmonary doctor and got some medication and that kept me out of the hospital in February 2009.

A few days later I received a call from the oncologist reporting that the PET scan detected nothing in my stomach and there was too much fluid in my lungs, so the test could not tell if anything was wrong. He told me he had scheduled an appointment with the Radiation oncologist for me. I responded with an okay and the conversation ended. When I placed the phone down I said to myself, "Why am I going to the Radiation oncologist when the test showed nothing." As far as I was concerned radiation needs a site to focus on. I had radiation when I had breast cancer and that was my interpretation. I really kept the appointment because the radiation oncologist was someone I could really talk with and he would be honest with me. My visit with the Radiation oncologist was exactly what I had expected. He was very honest about the situation. He made a call to my regular oncologist, but was unable to get in touch with him. He said he would give me a call if he heard from the oncologist. I thanked him and left his office.

When I got home I started making telephone calls. At that moment I

THE FACES OF STRUGGLES SUCH AS CANCERS
ARE ON THE JOURNEY TO GOD'S GLORY!

Alfancena Millicent Barrett

thanked God for television and advertisement. I was not willing to wait to hear from the oncologist. If you notice I changed from saying my oncologist to the oncologist because that was how I was feeling. I felt he just passed me over and did not come up with a treatment plan. Yes, he had treated me several times, but he was not God to think this was it for me. He did not say this in so many words, but that was my interpretation on the matter. I had a visit with my medical doctor, too; and he was somewhat concerned, but his respond was the oncologist was the expert. I thank God that I had insurance that could get me service across state lines. That made me wondered about those who do not have this privilege. I called several cancer centers in Philadelphia, and the local chapter of the Lymphoma Society in Wilmington. I asked if they knew an oncologist who specialized in lymphoma cancer. I was given the name of one doctor who worked out of the University of Pennsylvania (HUP). Two of the centers I called no one answered, so I left messages. I called the University of Pennsylvania and I was directed to the right person. The nurse took all my information over the phone and told me all I needed. The doctor who was recommended to me was booked until May 2009 and I felt that was too long because of the way I was feeling. I asked if there were other doctors who specialized in my kind of cancer. The answer was yes, and I was able to get an earlier appointment, but I did not confirm it. I wanted to talk to the other centers before I made up my mind. One of the other centers returned my call and while I was on the phone discussing my

THE FACES OF STRUGGLES SUCH AS CANCERS
ARE ON THE JOURNEY TO GOD'S GLORY!

Alfancena Millicent Barrett

situation the other center also returned my call. I asked the first one to hold, while I answered the other call. The second return call told me they needed to get my information and examined it first before it would go to the oncology department. So I said no thanks; when I returned to the first call the individual had hung up. I then said to myself, "The University of Penn it is," because I had already gotten an appointment date. I called the University and confirmed my appointment. I just believed that was where God was leading. I have never driven myself to Philadelphia and I had no idea exactly where I was going. I reflected on my favorite quote *"God will not lead you, where he will not provide for you."*

I started the process of collecting all my medical records since 2000 from two different hospitals. I had my medical doctor send his records to the University of Pennsylvania, also. All except one set of records was sent directly to the University of Pennsylvania; I had to pick that set up and deliver it myself. When I dropped the paper work off, it was said that they had more than enough material. March 2009 was the date of my first appointment with my new doctors and new cancer center. One of my dear church sisters who I was recently introduced to by my pastor's wife, offered to take me to my appointment. She herself was a survivor of Breast cancer and was living with Omental, a rare kind of cancer that they had not yet discovered a medication to administer treatment. That humbled me even more to know what she was going through, but found it no robbery to assist me. My friend had driven to Philadelphia before, but had not gone to this site. She had a Global Positioning Satellite (GPS) system; so we put in the address and started out on the journey. In spite of that, we did take the wrong exit and went in circles for a while, but we made it to the appointment. The next appointment she had a new GPS, which helped us better with our direction and by then I knew where we were going.

We got to the appointment, and I got registered. We waited in the waiting room with a group of other people and some appeared to be really sick. Very rare I have ever gone to a doctor's office and I looked sick. The waiting was long, but I often said that we pay to wait when we go to the doctor. I was very pleased with the attention I was given after that long wait. The doctor who saw me first was a fellowship doctor, which means she was still in training. She went over my health history with me thoroughly. We discussed the possibility for treatment. I was then seen by the official doctor. We had plans to check the status of my heart which could be damaged from treatment I received before; I had to see a pulmonary doctor to get my lungs checked; and blood work. I left the doctor's office very pleased and very hopeful. The long wait was worth it. The exit staff ensured me that I had all my appointments scheduled before I left the doctor's office. A couple of appointments were to precede my scheduled appointment with the oncology team, but when I checked after leaving the doctor's office I realized it was not so. I called the doctor's office the next day and the secretary was very kind; she got the

Alfancena Millicent Barrett

appointments changed so I was able to have all my tests and procedures done before my next appointment.

I gave God thanks that my heart was in good condition, which made it one step closer for me to be treated. The pulmonary doctor was very gentle and professional. She even walked me to the exit counter at the end of our session to get appointments schedule. I was very impressed that these folks walked the extra miles with their patients. I believe healing started right there and then, just from the initial treatment given by the University of Pennsylvania Perelman center staff. I had to schedule a pulmonary function test; this test identified my lung capacity. I had to do a high resolution CAT scan, also. I had many scans done, but never a high resolution one, I said to myself I am being introduced to a whole lot of new stuff. The pulmonary doctor discussed the best procedure to find out exactly what was going on with my lungs. It was either a biopsy or a bronchoscopy; of course I did not want to go for the biopsy because of my past experience. That was when she recommended the high resolution CAT scan. She also gave me a prescription to get a device which would help break up mucus from my lungs. I did not get the one on the prescription, but one similar called acapella. That device really worked. I believe that little device had kept me out of the hospital with pneumonia since then. It made me wonder that all the other pulmonary doctors I had seen before did not know about this device. They kept on giving me medication for asthma which did not prevent the pneumonia attacking me.

THE FACES OF STRUGGLES SUCH AS CANCERS
ARE ON THE JOURNEY TO GOD'S GLORY!

Alfancena Millicent Barrett

I am convinced if I had that device since 2005 I would not have paid so many visits to the hospital/hotel room.

The result of the pulmonary function test for my lungs indicated that I do not have full capacity of my lungs. I had the high resolution CAT scan done and the doctor reported that she had a better idea where to focus for the bronchoscopy. The bronchoscopy was scheduled. The staff that took care of me before and after the procedure were very caring. The day after the bronchoscopy procedure was my last day at work. I developed a temperature the same afternoon after the bronchoscopy. I did not call the doctor, I took some Tylenol and the fever went away that night. I wanted to feel better, because I wanted to be at work to be a part of "The Week of The Young Child Celebration." I spoke with my sister Delrose and she said there must have been some cancer cells that got disrupted which resulted in me getting a temperature. I had to agree with her, because I had this procedure done twice before and did not have any issue.

When I got up the next morning, I had no temperature, but I did not feel good either. I got my son off to school. I got myself ready and made it to work. As the minutes went by I kept feeling worse. My supervisor learned that I was not doing well and said I should go home. I wanted to at least see everyone got dressed and the conference room, the site for the event. You see, it was a very special time at our school and the theme for that year was "The Circus." One of my favorite things to do was to take pictures and I wanted a few pictures before going home. Right around the

THE FACES OF STRUGGLES SUCH AS CANCERS
ARE ON THE JOURNEY TO GOD'S GLORY!

Alfancena Millicent Barrett

time when everyone was ready to go to the celebration spot my back started to hurt and I could feel the chills returning. I went and got in my car, stopped by the site and witnessed the start of the celebration. I was there for approximately five minutes, I felt I was getting worse and I prayed I would make it home without any incident. Yes, thanks be to God I made it home, but it was very difficult to walk from the car to my front door. I was blessed that I had my nephew and his family living close by. I was even more blessed that he was home that day. When I made it inside I could not make it upstairs to get my breathing machine and I needed it to aid my breathing. I was able to call my nephew to come to my assistance. Even after the treatment I was still in pain, but I was able to make it upstairs to my bed. That was a frightening experience for me and all that happened in April of 2009.

I called my oncologist's office and told them what was going on. Some antibiotic was called into my pharmacy for me to start taking immediately. An appointment was scheduled for me to see the oncologist. The day of that appointment I learned when I was going to start treatment and what chemotherapy medication I was going to be given. I was given a few prescriptions for medication that I would be taking while going through treatment. This was the first time I was given so many medications. I found it reasonable, seeing that I was going to go through this for the fourth time. The medication for nausea, I told the doctor she did not have to prescribe that one because I never use it. She said she

THE FACES OF STRUGGLES SUCH AS CANCERS
ARE ON THE JOURNEY TO GOD'S GLORY!

Alfancena Millicent Barrett

would give me a few, just in case. I was able to say thanks be to God that still held true. I took one of those tablets by mistake, and the others were still on my kitchen counter in a container. I had never had a problem with nausea and never lost my appetite during chemotherapy treatment. That to me was a blessing all by itself. My first treatment started in May and each round of treatment would last over four days.

I was given Rituximab, Fludarabine and Cytoxan. The Rituximab had to be given slowly over several hours to avoid a reaction. I had to turn to some of the many people that God placed in my life to assist me with transportation. I had many who were very willing and able. I was very impressed with the staff at the front desk in my oncologist's office at the Perlman Center; I was called by name on my second visit. The day went pretty well, except when the nurse thought I was doing well with the medication and tried to speed it up. My throat started getting dry and I got shortness of breath. The nurse came and stopped it for awhile and then restarted it at the original pace. I made it through without any further incident. The other days of treatment went very well. I thought I was going to be tired, but instead the medication gave me more energy. I was doing everything around the house. It was about a week later before I was able to take a nap during the day; thank God I was able to sleep at night.

The following week after my first treatment I developed a temperature. I called my oncologist and she suggested I go to the emergency room and get checked out. I was given the antibiotic Vantin and was sent home. I had some other medications to take which I did. Shortly after I took the other medications my body became very painful. I went to bed shortly after that to see if I would feel better.

I woke up later that night to go to the bathroom and I felt light headed. I was blessed that one of my nephews from Jamaica was there with me. I walked to the bathroom and called out to him to come to my aid because I felt light headed. I remembered holding onto the bathroom sink, heard a noise and the next thing I knew I was waking up on the bathroom floor calling my nephew. He came and helped me up from the floor. He asked if I needed to go to the hospital; I said no because I was not feeling bad although I was still in pain. I went back to bed, but I was thinking how did I fall and end up in that position. I asked my nephew the following morning. He said he saw me fall, he tried to lift me, but I was too heavy. He placed me down and went to get the phone to call my other nephew who lived close by; it was at that point I woke up and called him. He said he was frightened and it was a little scary for me too because I had never experience that before. I guess unconsciousness is like dying for that moment, because only dead weight is difficult to handle. My nephew was strong enough to carry me around. I did call my oncologist the morning after and let her know what was going on. Although I was not feeling bad, I was still in pain. I asked my doctor if I could stop taking the other medications because I noticed I got painful after taking them. The doctor said the medications I am taking should not have that kind of reaction, but gave the okay and I noticed the pain got less.

On Saturday a day after taking none of the medication, I decided to call my nurse sister to discuss the medications. I decided to try the Dapsone again which was an antibiotic. Soon after I took it, I started to feel painful again. I called my oncologist and told her about my discovery. The doctor advised me to complete taking the Vantin before taking any more Dapsone. I have learned that medications work on people differently; everyone is not going to have the same reaction.

My second treatment had a rocky start because the center was making some changes. It made me discover how big the place really was; I had to go upstairs to another treatment room to get started. I was surprised how many treatment rooms the center accommodated. The treatment rooms at this center were state-of- the-art. Each patient has an individual room furnished with a recliner or a bed, television with remote, extra chairs for family members and a computer for the nurse's use. Individuals were welcome to close or have the door open while receiving treatment. My family member and I even received room service, yes we did; and it was done with a smile, too. We were asked to choose from a list of drinks and crackers. No wonder people talk about the good treatment at the University of Pennsylvania. My past experience was, everyone got treatment in one big room. I kept having a reaction to my Rituximab; because of the late start I only ended up getting half the treatment. My body was not accepting the faster pace of administration of the

THE FACES OF STRUGGLES SUCH AS CANCERS
ARE ON THE JOURNEY TO GOD'S GLORY!

Alfancena Millicent Barrett

medication. The rest of the week went well. I also received medication to help with my immune system. It sure helped because I did not get a temperature that time around.

Third treatment went very well, but the day after my treatment I should have gotten my special shot to help with my immune system, it was not possible because it was a holiday. I hoped that I would be okay until the following Monday. I was up and about that Friday after treatment. I even went to the grocery store; I wore a mask so I would be protected. Shortly after I returned home I started feeling a pain in my back and then I developed a temperature. I got in touch with my doctor the next day and the doctor advised me to go to the emergency room. I was hoping they would just treat me and send me home like the last time. Boy, was I wrong this time, it was my longest stay in the hospital. I spent nine days in the hospital and had to be transferred from one hospital to the next. My nuetropenia was low and they would not let me out of the hospital until it came back up to a safe level. With my nuetropenia level I was prone to infections. Although I was very comfortable at the first hospital, it did not make sense for me to stay, because my new oncology team was not able to see me in that hospital. That was one of my small fears; what would happen if I had to go to the hospital where I lived instead of the hospital where I am being treated. Lucky for me I did express this to my oncologist and she told me if that happened she would arrange to get me transferred.

I was in the first hospital from Saturday to Tuesday. When my medical

THE FACES OF STRUGGLES SUCH AS CANCERS

ARE ON THE JOURNEY TO GOD'S GLORY!

Alfancena Millicent Barrett

doctor did not discharge me Tuesday I made a phone call. The transfer was put in place just in case I was not given my marching orders on Wednesday morning. My doctor came, but was not sending me home so I told him about the backup plan, to which he agreed. My transfer was an interesting one; I learned from the nurse on duty that everything was ready for me to be transferred, but she was waiting to hear about transportation. That took forever and when the nurse finally reappeared she told me that I was not sick enough for the insurance to pay for transportation and neither would the hospital. I found that very interesting and I was not well enough to go home either. I was so blessed that one of my friends who came to visit with me earlier was still in the area and was able to take me to the next hospital. The nurse was very sweet too, she personally walked with me to the pickup area and waited with me until my ride came. I did appreciate that personal attention and I was happy to know that she cared.

At the other hospital which was the University of Pennsylvania, my room was ready and waiting for me. My friend dropped me off at the entrance and I was able to find my way with the help of the personnel at the front desk. My friend was unable to walk with me, because parking is not cheap at the University of Pennsylvania. As I mentioned before I called all my hospital visits my vacation spot, but my room at the University of Pennsylvania was state-of-the-art. My room had hard wood floors, I had a refrigerator, reclining chair which could be as a bed if someone was staying overnight with the patient and a television. Two

THE FACES OF STRUGGLES SUCH AS CANCERS
ARE ON THE JOURNEY TO GOD'S GLORY!

Alfancena Millicent Barrett

things I missed on this visit were the beautiful sceneries and I could not watch what I wanted on the television after the first day without a cost. My room was surrounded by other buildings. The amazing thing about looking at those buildings was the workmanship and their creative history. I was always appreciative of the services I received at the other hospitals, but so far the University of Pennsylvania topped them all. The first hospital I used to go to the service was good, but they could no longer, in my opinion, cater to my needs. I had difficulty being in a room with someone else, especially if that person could not take care of their own needs. I understood it would be difficult for that hospital because it was small and primarily privately run. I told my medical doctor the next time I have to go to the hospital I am going to the next hospital in my town and he was okay with that. The only thing I did not like was that I would be seen by his partner more than I would see him.

Boy, did I relish in the attention that was given to me at the University of Pennsylvania! Everyone was so pleasant and appeared to be very caring. I thought I was only going to spend one night to be checked out, I ended up staying four nights. My stay on that visit was one of pleasant memories. First I was seen by a team of young student doctors and they too had hopes that I might be going home the next day. The next morning when they returned with the head doctor I learned my fate. I was still in a danger zone to get sick so I was not able to go home. Later that day, I learned that I would not be seen by that team anymore; I was too well for that team; I was now going to be seen by the practitioner team. I found that so amusing, here I go again, I was too well for one group, but too sick to go home. I had a good time sharing my story with some of the young nurses. I shared my story with one of the nurses about how I started getting treatment here in Pennsylvania. I told her I went through the same thing in 2008, but apparently that treatment did not take care of the problem. I said to her if that treatment had worked I would not have been given the opportunity to meet her. She responded "You are right and I am happy I got the chance to meet you." When the nurse left my room, I reflected on our conservation; when we live in God's will there is no need to be depressed about the things we go through in life because we never know his purpose in all of it. God can use any situation and circumstances to draw people to Him. Some of the nurses expressed that they wish all their patients were like me, but I pray upon reflection they would realize that I am the patient I am because of my faith in God. I was never afraid to let them know it was never about me, but it was all about God.

Four days later I was able to go home. Would you believe it if I tell you that shortly after I got home I had a temperature. That evening I placed it all in God's hands because I was not prepare to go back to the hospital. I did not call that moment like I should; I went to bed and the temperature got lower. The next morning it was totally gone by the afternoon. I sure gave God thanks that I was spared from going to the hospital. When we first set up the treatment plan it was a possibility I was going through four to six rounds of treatments. My doctor's visit before my fourth treatment, my doctors scheduled PET scan appointment sometime after my fourth treatment, and they told me if everything looked good I would do no more treatments, but if not, they would keep going even though my bone marrow was complaining. I found that real funny. To God be the glory, I only had four treatments. Now, it was time for the real healing to take place, which hopefully will have me returning to the work force sooner than later.

CHAPTER 13

I THOUGHT THE TEST WAS OVER

Sometimes I feel like Job, I know I have not lived the life of Job, but every time I am on the road to recovery something else comes up. One month after my fourth, treatment I started having sores in my mouth. I went to the dentist and was sent to the specialist. He said it appeared that it was the after effect of the chemo, and that was good news. The sores would not heal and as a result I ended up in the hospital again because I developed a temperature that would not go away. All the tests at the hospital came back negative and with medication the temperature went away. My mouth started healing, but it appeared I needed more antibiotics. Luckily for me, I had an appointment with the dentist. I told him I went to the hospital as a result of the sores in my mouth and it started healing with the antibiotic they had given me. He prescribed antibiotic, one more related to my mouth issue. At the end of the medication, my mouth was healed. Two weeks later my mouth broke out into sores again and this time it was very painful. Delrose, my nurse sister said it could be caused from stress. I am not one to get stressed easily, but there was a situation in my home which I believe caused it.

My interpretation of the situation, when the devil cannot get you one way, he will try another. The devil's goal in our lives is to mess up our

THE FACES OF STRUGGLES SUCH AS CANCERS
ARE ON THE JOURNEY TO GOD'S GLORY!

Alfancena Millicent Barrett

testimonies. The more you have a closer relationship with God the harder he tires. At times he brings the fight to you in your home among your family and friends. The devil's job is to test every link and where there is weakness that is where he will try to break through, if he can't find one, he will try to break through your strength. In my case, I believed the devil said to himself, I have been attacking her body and I just can't win her over; I am going to try and attack her through one of her strengths.

I had mentioned before that my experiences coming to the United States were wonderful ones; God provided someone on every corner to supply my every need. My friend's daughter, who was in Jamaica and wanted to return to the United States to pursue a college education, needed somewhere to start out. I invited her to stay with me because I had the accommodation. I was so very excited because I was going to be given the opportunity to give this individual some of the great treatment I received. The strangest thing happened two nights after her arrival, I went to bed and dreamt about fire coming from the room where she was sleeping. I knew what that dream of fire meant, that spells trouble. My ex-husband often told me I should write a dream book. He had witnessed some of the dreams I had come to pass. I did not think there were enough dreams for a book, so I never did. Now I am getting the opportunity to share some of my dreams with you. When I woke up from that dream, I said, "Lord, that means trouble and if so why did you allow it?" I had to draw upon my faith, prayed and left it in God's hands. My experiences had thought me

THE FACES OF STRUGGLES SUCH AS CANCERS
ARE ON THE JOURNEY TO GOD'S GLORY!

Alfancena Millicent Barrett

that God had not led me to any situation that He had not walked with me.

I did discover the kind of trouble I was in for. The first weekend with my house guest and the way she communicated with me I thought to myself, it appeared everything was going to be fine. One part of my house guest's plan was to get a job before looking about school. I gave her ideas where she could get a job and the free reign of my computer to assist with her job search. I was very excited for her when soon after she got some interviews. Even though I was going through chemotherapy treatment, I provided her transportation to the interviews. Short distances, I would take her myself and long distances, my nephew, who was visiting, would do the driving. I took her to the first interview and on the return trip I was taken aback when she did not say thank you. I kept that to myself, but later realized it was a habit after many trips. The first time I received a "thank you" was after I spoke with her mother. A few weeks after her arrival she would not communicate with me and her changed personality made it difficult for me to reach out to her.

In spite of all that, I opened heart and resources to make her comfortable. I found it hard that someone living in my house that I treated as a family, treated me like a stranger. On one occasion when I tried talking to her about my disappointments she responded that it often take her time to warm up to people. I found that interesting because that was not how she started out and she was able to communicate with most of the people who visited my home. My friends and family were upset about the

THE FACES OF STRUGGLES SUCH AS CANCERS
ARE ON THE JOURNEY TO GOD'S GLORY!

Alfancena Millicent Barrett

situation and wanted me to ask her to leave. They were concerned that this individual would cause my recovery to be delayed. In times like those I witnessed the awesomeness of God's grace and mercy. I was really amazed that the atmosphere did not affect me psychologically as it could have done. Throughout all that, I felt very peaceful. Would you believe it with that situation, I welcomed another individual in my home that needed a helping hand.

My second house guest was from another state and wanted to try my state to try her luck at getting a job. We had discussed this matter earlier in the year, 2009. It did not materialize within the time frame we had discussed because she decided to go elsewhere. Sometime later my second guest called and asked if she could still come by because it wasn't working out where she was. I said yes, because I never wanted to miss an opportunity to help someone else. My life has been blessed by other people's kindness. It was a difficult moment to say yes, because I was terminated from my job as result of being on long term disability (LTD). My faith in God gave me the assurance, if God allowed her to come by; He would make the necessary provision. I was in the hospital and did not hear my cell phone ring. I checked the message; it was a message from my second house guest that she was coming that day. I did not even call the people who were at my house at the time to inform them, because I was expecting a call that she was on her way. The called I received was that she was at my door.

THE FACES OF STRUGGLES SUCH AS CANCERS
ARE ON THE JOURNEY TO GOD'S GLORY!

Alfancena Millicent Barrett

I had to let the people at my house know it was okay to allow her in. I came home later that week from the hospital. My first weekend home from the hospital gave me some warning signs that my second house guest might not be around long. She wanted me to prepare breakfast for her. I told her she knew she was welcome to use everything in my house, but I would not take on that responsibility. Now this individual is much older and healthier than I am and in my thinking she should be telling me to go relax and let her fix the breakfast. I trust you got the picture I am painting. That was just one of the stories and it would take another book just to tell you the others.

I was still willing to give her the chance she asked for. Two weeks later the atmosphere in my house became stressful and as a result I had to take action. A conflict arose between myself and my second guest; when I tried to address it, I was stunned by the response. One reason was because I had spoken to her earlier that week addressing issues which would avoid conflict when people share accommodation. The moment I opened my mouth, I was attacked with words. In summary, I had no right to be upset. One statement was that I was too thin skinned. One of the statements that made me realize I had to stand by my words was when I asked her to leave, she attacked my Christianity. She implied that because I am a Christian I should not have taken the action I pursued. I believe some folks forget as Christians we are still human and as a Christian serving God truthfully, one can't do so in an environment of strife. As a Christian we

THE FACES OF STRUGGLES SUCH AS CANCERS
ARE ON THE JOURNEY TO GOD'S GLORY!

Alfancena Millicent Barrett

still have the power to free ourselves of things that are stumbling blocks, it was hard for me to ask her to leave, but it had to be done for my peace of mind and health.

The weeks before she left it reinforced in my life how God's peace was with me. We only communicated about things that were necessary. I personally felt if we could not deal with the first conflict that happened, there was no reason to pretend everything was well. The two people that I opened my home to at a time when it was difficult for me to do so, joined forces against me. If you were a fly on the wall you would think I was the uninvited guest. I did find it amusing that my first house guest who after two months had difficulty communicating with me; but found it no problem being buddies with the second house guest. My friends and relatives who were witnesses of the situation were very upset. Through that storm, God kept me cool and collective. Somehow during the final week of this ordeal, the first guest started directing her anger at me which I felt within my bones. It was an experience that was very frightening; I could not believe that anger from someone else could have such physical implication. My friends willingly came by to join in a discussion to let my house guests understand how their behavior was affecting my health. It so happened I had only asked one guest to leave, but the other one ended up leaving the following week. I smiled and said to myself "I guess the purpose of my second guest was to hasten the departure of my first guest."

I was able to look back and be reminded of the song, "*Through it all I*

THE FACES OF STRUGGLES SUCH AS CANCERS ARE ON THE JOURNEY TO GOD'S GLORY!

Alfancena Millicent Barrett

have learned to trust in Jesus" and one of the scripture verses from my car's daily bread box. The scripture verse was from Deuteronomy 33:25b *"As thy days, so shall thy strength be."* That was a verse I first read one morning on my way to work while I was separated from my ex-husband; that morning I got into a car accident trying to pass a garbage truck on a one way street. I was puzzled by those words when I read them and was even more puzzled when I got in the accident. It is a verse that will stay with me, because God allows us to go through events in our life to make us stronger. That gave me the assurance once my life is in God's hands; everything and I mean everything that takes place in my life was done in God purpose. The purpose of God's often resulted in God receiving HIS GLORY!

CHAPTER 14

AGENTS OF GOD'S GLORY

When The Door Bell Rang is the title of one of my favorite children's books. During my struggles the sound of my door bell became a heartwarming tune because of who was on the other side of my door. Often times there were church sisters or brothers, friends, or family members bearing gifts. I came to the realization that these folks were agents of God's glory. There were agents who did not ring the door bell, but they sent cards which I could tell were specially handpicked. Some card did not come with just words of love, but gifts of love, too. Those were the things that made my faith grow stronger because through them I witnessed the promises of God.

The following promises kept me going and growing during my time in the valleys: "*But my God shall supply all your needs according to his riches in glory by Christ Jesus*" Philippians 4:19; "*Be of good courage, and he shall strengthen your heart, all ye that hope in the Lord*" Psalm 31: 24; "*Behold, I am with thee, and will keep thee in all places whither thou goest, and will bring thee again into the land (bring me back to health); for I will not leave thee, until I have done that which I have spoken to thee of*" Genesis 28:15. It was even more powerful when He used the agents He sent in my time of need to fulfill each promise. The simplest of gifts I

THE FACES OF STRUGGLES SUCH AS CANCERS
ARE ON THE JOURNEY TO GOD'S GLORY!

Alfancena Millicent Barrett

received was appreciated because I accepted each as a gift from God. Also, knowing others care so much was medicine to my ailing body.

I remembered the first time I came in close contact with one of my church sisters, she said to me, "You are Alfancena, I always pray for you." When she said those words to me, I felt special and blessed. Having someone sending up earnest prayers for me without even knowing who I was, to me that was the power of God flowing through His people. Some gifts I received were cooked meal or food to prepare a meal. I remembered growing up listening to gospel services on the radio or reading in a book of people giving testimonies of how God provided for them in times of need. Their needs would be met by someone bringing food or money that they had prayed for, but had no idea when and how it would be delivered. They would go to their mailbox, open an envelope and find money. As a child I thought that sounded good, but was that really true? I am able to say today that God still answers prayers just the same; which reinforces the words in Hebrews 13:8, "*Jesus Christ the same yesterday, and today, and forever.*" I too have gone to my mailbox and received gifts in that manner or it was delivered in person.

The spring of 2009, one of my neighbors who knew my love of the garden, gathered flowering plants for my garden. She did not only gathered the plants, she got another neighbor to join her in planting them. It was heartwarming to watch them digging with garden shovels and bending to put the plants in the ground. All I could quietly say to myself,

THE FACES OF STRUGGLES SUCH AS CANCERS
ARE ON THE JOURNEY TO GOD'S GLORY!

Alfancena Millicent Barrett

"God is an awesome God." People took time out of their busy schedule to bless me in ways that were unexpected. I have two house plants that were given to me during the first and second time I got diagnosed with cancer that have grown and flourished so much that I have often time compared my life with them; especially when I did not water them for a while and they continued to flourish. Even though my body has been attacked so many times by cancer, friends and family often commented about the smile on my face. I often marveled at how I was able to sing God's praises with damaged lungs whenever I am in His house with His people. I also believe those plants flourish because of the spirit of love in which they were given to me.

My neighbors would ensure that my lawn was well manicured in the summer, free of leaves in the fall and clear pathway free from snow in the winter. The blessed thing was the enthusiasm they performed the task. My neighbor who I could call to remove a squirrel from my house, did not hesitate and he was at my door in no time to tackle the tedious assignment he was given. My dear friends were always ready and willing to drive me to my doctors' appointment; especially ones who were dealing with their own fight with sickness. One of my dear sisters took it upon herself to ensure I received a box of food from church each month. I mentioned this because even after she suffered a stroke and was unable to get my box of food, she showed concern. The healing of God's hands came not only through medication, but also through the people He placed in my path.

THE FACES OF STRUGGLES SUCH AS CANCERS
ARE ON THE JOURNEY TO GOD'S GLORY!

Alfancena Millicent Barrett

At times I wondered why I was always on the receiving end. God used His agents to bless me. At times I desired to give back in a tangible way, but was unable to do so. Then I seriously thought about it; and the question came, would I be as humble as I am now if I was able to give back at my own freewill? The answer came to me, maybe not. Therefore I believe God placed me in the position He wanted me to serve and I was even more humbled by that thought. The love God bestowed upon me through His agents made me have no time to mope, but every moment to hope. Like Paul in 2Corinthians 12:7-9, I could say, ***"Lest I should be exalted above measure through the abundance of the revelations, there was given to me a thorn in the flesh, the messenger of Satan to buffet me, lest I should be exalted above measure. For this thing I besought the Lord thrice, that it might depart from me."*** God answered, ***"My grace is sufficient for thee: for my strength is made perfect in weakness. Most gladly therefore will I rather glory in my infirmities, that the power of Christ may rest upon me."*** Again I say "God is an awesome God" and I live as a witness to His **GLORY!**

CHAPTER 15

CONTRIBUTION FROM THE PEOPLE GOD PLACED IN MY PATH ON THIS JOURNEY

From My Sister-in-law Rosanna Barrett:

My sister-in-law Millicent is the most optimistic person I have ever met. Even when we expressed concerns about her illnesses (several episodes of cancers) she would always have a cheerful statement of hope. Throughout her struggles with cancer she never complained and was amazingly more concerned about the health and well being of others. She was always comforting telling us not to worry, she would be fine. She is always helping others, reaching beyond her own limitations to help family members, friends and even strangers. She is always willing to fix a problem, offering a listening ear; sound words of advice and encouragement; and continuous words of prayers and comfort. Throughout her illnesses she was always smiling with gracious countenance and a face full of joy no one would imagine the pain she must had endured from just looking at her physical appearance. Her strong faith in God is remarkable. A faith that most Christians strive towards. Instead of feeling sorry and angry about her illnesses, she kept saying "God has me here for a reason and He will not take me until I have accomplished that purpose."

THE FACES OF STRUGGLES SUCH AS CANCERS
ARE ON THE JOURNEY TO GOD'S GLORY!

Alfancena Millicent Barrett

She is an inspiration to me and my family. Every time I caught myself complaining about a pain or some minor illness I remember her resilience after she had been through so much and would feel so ungrateful and unappreciative of my blessing. She is a rock of hope and a pillar of perseverance. We are truly blessed by God to have her as a part of our family. The legacy of faith she represents will continue to grow and live in our hearts forever.

From My Sister in Christ Ruth Wilson:

My friend, Alfancena, "Spread love everywhere you go: first of all in your own house...let no one ever come to you without leaving better and happier. Be the living expression of God's kindness in your face, kindness in your eyes, and kindness in your warm greeting." - *Mother Teresa*

Sometimes God throws us a lifeline when we need it the most. That is my first and lasting impression of my dear friend, former co-worker and sister in Christ, Alfancena. I met Alfancena around mid 1996 during one of my days working as a computer instructor at Delaware Technical and Community College, Wilmington campus. She was always in the computer lab diligently working on her assigned projects. One day she asked me for assistance while she was beginning to work in the MS Access software. I took the time to explain the procedures to her; she graciously thanked me in such a way that you would have thought that I had just saved her life.

THE FACES OF STRUGGLES SUCH AS CANCERS
ARE ON THE JOURNEY TO GOD'S GLORY!

Alfancena Millicent Barrett

As sisters in Christ we encountered each other frequently and when she was diagnosed with her first cancer, I was informed. One day I received a call from Alfancena needing my assistance to go to a doctor's appointment. After receiving that phone call I realized that God had brought us together for a reason. I also wondered why she called and there and then the spirit spoke to me in a soft whispered voice, "Because she needed you." That moment also revealed to me another purpose God had for my life. I have been there through all of her battles with cancers and her divorce and I had never met anyone like Alfancena. Not once did she ever cry or say I am afraid, or why cancer had found its way to my body. As I watched her, her faith, strength, and trust in God grew deeper and stronger each day.

Whenever I am in her presence, I could feel the arms of healing reaching me during my own pains and sickness. She helped me to put difficult times in my life into perspective and to increase my own faith. Those of us who know Alfancena, we can truly say that her demonstration of her walk with God has inspired us to live each day as we were created to do. She is a living testimony for all who have come to know her. To God be all glory, Honor, and Praise.

From My Sister in Christ Margaret Johnson (Mom):

"STANDING ON FAITH" Deaconess Alfancena is truly a perfect example of an individual "Standing on Faith."

THE FACES OF STRUGGLES SUCH AS CANCERS
ARE ON THE JOURNEY TO GOD'S GLORY!

Alfancena Millicent Barrett

Alfancena, a child of the King, is a living testimony to anyone that had cancer. The doctors of this world had diagnosed her with three cancers, but oh no, the true doctor that Alfancena knows brought her through all three. She cannot stop praising God enough for all that He had done and is still doing for her.

"Standing on Faith" Alfancena is a warm and loving person. She always greet people with a smile on her face. She never complained or griped about her condition. She would tell you that everything was in God's hand and she will be alright- now that is what I call, "Standing On faith."

She affectionately calls me Mom and I am honored to be referred to as her mom. I am proud to know Alfancena, she has truly been an inspiration to all of us.

From My Sister in Christ Joan Hodge-Roberts:

Tribute to Alfancena - A Christian, a true believer, filled with the Holy Spirit; how else could she have survived without the spirit of GOD in her life- HE IS HER LIFE!!! Alfancena is an ANGEL on earth, caring, compassionate, and loving. Thank you Alfancena for your inspiration and love you have given me.

From My Brother in Christ Percival McNeil:

The song writer penned, "Many things about tomorrow I don't seem to understand; but I know who holds tomorrow and I know who holds my

THE FACES OF STRUGGLES SUCH AS CANCERS
ARE ON THE JOURNEY TO GOD'S GLORY!
Alfancena Millicent Barrett

hands." These words of the song express the belief and character of my sister Alfancena. Although you have been struck with three different cancers, and always seem to be battling the ever present effects of the treatments and residual elements, you show no sign of discouragement, bitterness or fear. You are always smiling and giving thanks to God for the moment of life, an attitude that gives strength to me and many others. Your favorite words, "God has a purpose for me, not yet fulfilled," bring comfort and optimism to all around you. The truth in your words can be validated from the number of people (including my sister, Veronica), who have passed on although they were diagnosed after you. Your strength and humility are Christian qualities that every believer should aspire to imitate. I know your confidence can only be attributed to your deep abiding faith in Jesus Christ and the realization that you are only a pilgrim passing though this land unto your permanent home not made with earthly hands. Continue to be a light in this world of darkness.

From My Sister in Christ Deaconess Dorenda Boger:

Sister Alfancena Davis and I serve as fellow deaconesses working in God's vineyard. For the past five years we have shared some really high spiritual moments together. I have also witnessed her struggles with sickness going in and out of the hospital. Whenever I would visit her in the hospital she often made me laugh when she related her hospital experiences as a vacation spot, such as the Hilton hotel.

THE FACES OF STRUGGLES SUCH AS CANCERS ARE ON THE JOURNEY TO GOD'S GLORY!

Alfancena Millicent Barrett

The smile Sister Alfancena wears would melt one's heart and she has the strength of a lion. My family and I have become very fond of her.

From My Friend Lydia Miller:

Faith: A word that is only as strong as one's love for the Lord. Faith can only be tested in times of trouble or despair; some have it, some don't. My dear friend Alfancena has it.

I met Alfancena in the summer of 1996. We got to know each other on both a professional and friendly basis where she quickly became a mentor. I found her to be a very warm and intellectual young lady. I learned that she held fast to what a Christian should be. Regardless of the harshness or severity of the circumstances that may have surrounded her, her faith was evident.

I have been there since the year 2000 when she was first diagnosed with Lymphoma cancer; then later in the year 2003 she was diagnosed with breast cancer and in 2006 was diagnosed with uterine cancer. Through the strength and blessings of the Lord, from 2000 through 2008, Alfancena was able to overcome them all. However, in the year 2009, Alfancena strength of faith was tested again with the return of lymphoma cancer. It had returned with intense aggression. Sometimes she would become so ill, that I would start to cry and she would say, "God is not ready for me yet; my task has not been completed." And although her doctor had given up on her, she never gave up on the Lord. She continued

THE FACES OF STRUGGLES SUCH AS CANCERS
ARE ON THE JOURNEY TO GOD'S GLORY!

Alfancena Millicent Barrett

seeking help and the Lord lead her to the University of Pennsylvania, Perelman Medical Center. She is a true living testimony of what the good Lord can do if you believe.

Looking at cancer through the eyes of my friend, Alfancena, and how she relied on her relationship with the Lord caused my faith to be renewed. With awesome faith she often states, "No matter what may come my way dear Lord, my life is in your hands." I had other love ones who had succumbed to this illness, Alfancena would respond by saying, "I am alive today because He kept me by His grace and mercy and I will never let go." The warmth and compassion from her soul illuminated through her eyes even though at times her body ached; provided me with great comfort and peace.

Proverbs 31:10, states *"Who can find a virtuous woman, for her price is far above rubies;"* well, I can say I am blessed to have found that virtuous woman, whose price is far above rubies…in my friend, Alfancena Barrett-Davis.

From My Friend Jonnie Smith:

When I met my friend affectionately called Miss Barrett she was in the mist of her battle with cancer. If our good friend Lydia did not tell me I would not have known. She was full of joy and happiness. I was always amazed at her high spirits and peace. My theory is that everyone has something positive to give from their experiences, and that you can gain strength through other people's battles. When she felt that one doctor had given up on her as she faced the challenge of a returning cancer, she solicited help from another hospital in a nearby state. I call it a challenge because she would always said the battle is not mine it's the Lord's.

It was mentioned to me that she needed rides to her treatments I jumped at the opportunity to assist her. It may sound selfish but I wanted to see firsthand this strong unfailing faith she held fast to. Each time I picked her up instead of her looking weaker she appeared stronger. Instead of her hair falling out it got thicker, and instead of her becoming thinner she seemed healthier. She is a true example of a faithful virtuous woman. Her faith had brought her this far standing on the promises of God. Holding fast to His Word that He will never leave her nor forsake her and that He is that unfailing present help in the time of trouble.

From My Sister in Christ Ingrid Price:

Now Faith is the substance of things hoped for, the evidence of things not seen. Hebrews 11:1

We, as professed Christians, can quote this scripture all too well, but if we are being true to its real meaning, our Faith in our Lord and Savior should not and cannot be hampered by the trials and tribulations in our lives and the lives of those with whom we find ourselves closely connected.

THE FACES OF STRUGGLES SUCH AS CANCERS
ARE ON THE JOURNEY TO GOD'S GLORY!

Alfancena Millicent Barrett

As we journey through life here on earth, we can rest assured, knowing that our Faith will undoubtedly be tested time and time again, as mine has been over the years, through the loss of my mother, Josephine, from breast cancer just before her 56 birthday; my sister, Janet, being diagnosed with breast cancer three years ago, and then lung cancer two years later; and my 42 year old niece, Felice, the mother of a 2-year old, diagnosed with stage 3 colon cancer three months ago. I must admit, my Faith has wavered over the years as I wrestled, time and time again, with the question of "why is God allowing this to happen to my loved ones?" yet, in spite of my response to His tests of my Faith, He has seen fit to place His "archangel", Sister Alfancena Davis, in my life to expose me to such a beautiful-spirited person who has endured the pain and hardship of a breast cancer diagnosis, lymphoma, and a uterine cancer diagnosis, compounded by the loss of her mother, her brother, sister-in-law, and father during her period of affliction, yet she never seemed to lose Faith in our Lord and Savior, and the plans that He has for her here on earth. Sister Alfancena is the epitome of Faith, and she consistently demonstrates through her attitude and actions the magnanimous hope and trust in God that He expects from those of us who profess ourselves to be Christians.

Sister Alfancena has not only been a genuine spiritual partner and Sister-in-Christ to me, but she has also extended her love and support to my sisters, Janet and Vivian, who have come to love her just as much as I. We thank you for being the person that God has intended for you to be.

THE FACES OF STRUGGLES SUCH AS CANCERS ARE ON THE JOURNEY TO GOD'S GLORY!

Alfancena Millicent Barrett

I hope and pray that Sister Alfancena's "Story" will have the same profound effect of strengthening others' Faith as it has had on the strengthening of my Faith.

Being confident of this very thing, that He which hath begun a good work in you will perform it until the day of Jesus Christ. Philippians 1:6

From My Friend Karen Green:

Your faith, strength and perseverance is proof that you are a child of God and that He takes care of His children. For that I thank you for being the best friend I ever had and making me believe more and more in Him each day. God bless you my angel and dearest friend.

From My Friend Rebecca Freeman (Ms. Becky):

Ms. Alfie, as she is affectionately called is a beautiful black lady of great faith in God.

She has been an inspiration to me and those in her surroundings. I had the pleasure of meeting Ms. Alfie while being a student at Delaware Technical and Community College, while pursuing a diploma in Early Childhood Development. While attending the college, I was employed by the Early Childhood Development Center under the leadership of Ms. Alfie. I learned much, about the care of children, from her guidance. We often spoke of the love of God and His awesome power during our lunches and breaks. Ms. Alfie was recovering from cancer when I met her.

THE FACES OF STRUGGLES SUCH AS CANCERS
ARE ON THE JOURNEY TO GOD'S GLORY!

Alfancena Millicent Barrett

Two years later cancer invaded her body once again. Ms. Alfie's faith has sustained her and we have prayed daily for her, putting our faith and Trust in God and He has blessed her tremendously.

From My Sister in Christ Deaconess Irma Parker:

For the past eight and a half years I've known Alfancena to be a person with a very strong faith in God. I've seen her go through many battles with cancer and each time I see her, she always has a smile on her face. No matter how much pain she is in, you can see on her face that she is trusting God.

She is always saying that God has her here for a reason. I can truly say that one of the reasons she is here, is to help me grow my faith in God. Alfancena is a person that would go out of her way to help you. She would give you an uplifting word when you are down. God has His hands on her life and He has His angel watching over her.

I like to leave you with Matthew 4:4, It is written, "Man shall not live by bread alone, but by every word that proceeds from the mouth of God." If you know Alfancena, then you know that she lives by the word of God.

From My Friend Barbara Sheppard-Taylor:

The year was 1999, I had just been hired as a member of the faculty at the Delaware Technical and Community College. I was sitting at my desk reviewing course materials in preparation for my classes, when this very

THE FACES OF STRUGGLES SUCH AS CANCERS

ARE ON THE JOURNEY TO GOD'S GLORY!

Alfancena Millicent Barrett

quiet speaking, tall slim lady appeared at the office door. She was asking to speak to Mr. Stewart, my office mate, in reference to a position at our newly opened Child Development Center. He introduced me to Ms. Alfie, as she is affectionately called by her friends and others who know her. This was the first of my interactions I would have with this wonderful caring person.

Ms. Alfie was hired as the lead teacher for the infant classroom. My position required me to visit the CDC frequently so I had the opportunity to develop a relationship with her. One of the things I recognized about her, was her devotion to providing the absolute best care for the babies in her classroom. Everything in her classroom had to be just so, and if you didn't abide by the high standard she set for herself and others, you would hear it from Ms. Alfie. That was why the parents absolutely adored her and trusted her with their most prized possessions, their babies.

Ms. Alfie became ill and everyone was so concerned for her, and who was going to care for their infants. Her reputation was known throughout the college, faculty, staff and students who had the privilege of leaving their babies in her care, they found out it was one of the best decisions they could make. Even when she was ill, one of her only thoughts was what about my babies, for she treated them like they were her very own. She would come in to visit or call the center to check on them, or maintain contact with the parents just to make sure everything was all right.

So what kind of person is Ms. Alfie? She is a caring person, not only for the care she gives her babies, but others. She is a devoted person, devoted to doing the very best she can, even when she was ill, tired and weak. She is a godly person, for her faith in GOD has been her strength and her belief has sustained her through all the things.

I sincerely love Ms. Alfie; I am grateful and thankful to God for allowing me to know her. For I believe that she is a "phenomenal woman" who will stand for what's right and give the gallant fight with all she has to give.

From My Sister Florence Burton:

"What a fellowship, what a joy divine." Alfie and I are not just neighbors, not just friends, we're not just sister cancer survivors, but we are sisters in Christ sharing the same faith, the same hope in knowing that we are more than survivors, we are victorious in Christ Jesus. Coming through some very serious health issues God has blessed the both of us.

Knowing that cancer like sin when ignored, because we do not exam ourselves on regular basis, will kill you. But when attention is being paid to one's self and cancer or sin is detected early and we take steps that lead to eradication, then we are more than likely to be doing the victory dance. No matter what battles Alfie has gone through she remains an uplifting, inspirational, encouraging, and a light to all who come across her path.

THE FACES OF STRUGGLES SUCH AS CANCERS
ARE ON THE JOURNEY TO GOD'S GLORY!

Alfancena Millicent Barrett

From My Friend and Parent Nicole Harris:

I met Alfancena (Ms. Alfie) in early 2000. She was working at Deltech Early Childhood Development Center where I had enrolled my one year-old son Devon. Ms. Alfie was Devon's teacher and care provider. She loved Devon and took very good care of him and we grew to love her as well. Month-to-month, it was sometimes a struggle to pay to keep Devon at Deltech, but I knew that he was receiving phenomenal care with Ms. Alfie's patient hands and loving heart. She told me one day that Devon was the busiest child that she had ever had and we laughed. I want you to know Ms. Alfie that he has not changed even at age 10! Well after Devon had left the school, and we moved to Georgia and now Ohio, your love, your conversation and your life has continued to touch me and reach a dwelling in me that virtually no one else has ever found. I know it has been a long road for you with tremendous struggles, but you never, ever complain. How do you do that? Your love for God and others and your courage is incomparable to none. Thank you for encouraging me, for listening to me, for praying for me and Devon and allowing me to know you for myself. If you never knew before, I want you to know now that you are a very special person to me and a precious gift from God to so many others. You are MY Ms. Alfie, MY friend, MY hero! I love you. Congratulations on the book - Congratulations on YOU!"

THE FACES OF STRUGGLES SUCH AS CANCERS
ARE ON THE JOURNEY TO GOD'S GLORY!

Alfancena Millicent Barrett

From My Pastor Reverend Dr. Clifford I. Johnson:

While everyone will experience setbacks in life there are certain people that find themselves in a gulf of trials and even spiritual let downs. In these moments we hear a lot about Job and there is a tendency to refer to him in discussions with people that are experiencing occurrences that seem so overwhelming. From an intellectual standpoint there are persons that talk about Job, but how often in real life do we meet an individual with the faith, courage, and fortitude of him? It is most important for this generation to encounter such a person for there is a desire to see the evidence of who God is and what God does. I along with many am blessed for we have the privilege of meeting Alfancena Davis, a woman of faith.

Alfancena's faith has been the source of encouragement for many people that have encountered her. On so many occasions, there have been people that were about to give up. After meeting Alfancena and feeling her strength, they were encouraged to fight on with a sense of endurance and belief that God would send the change.

Alfancena has a faith that begins inside and radiates outside to the point where it becomes infectious. It is not possible to meet Alfancena and not see her smile of courage and not know that in spite of your condition help is on the way. God has a purpose for her life and it is being fulfilled on a daily basis. Men and women in society are searching for their purpose in life. It is a blessing to meet someone that has discovered what that purpose is and after doing so, spends their time living it out. Further, it is a blessing to see the scriptures in living color. Alfancena is faith in action.

Author's Final Thoughts:

I give God thanks for what He allowed folks to see Jesus through me. I pray for humility to do His will. Yes, with all the strength demonstrated there were times when I got overwhelm, but then I found it ironic when they who witnessed those moments they reacted in surprise as if that should not be. It was because of the love and support I received from everyone that made those moments rare. GLORY BE TO GOD THROUGH JESUS.

CHAPTER 16

WORDS OF LOVE FROM ME TO YOU THE READERS

It is important that we take care of our bodies, 1 Corinthians 6:19, let us know it is God's temple. We need to eat right and exercise. Know your body that when something is wrong you know; that was one of my saving graces. I always knew when something was not right. Do your annual checkup; visit your doctor when things are not feeling right, without delay. It is better to hear the words "it is nothing", than to hear the words, " it's too far gone." For those who have no health insurance I pray that will change one day, but until then, there are free services for areas such as Breast cancer and Prostate cancer screening. Inform yourself about diseases that can attack the body. For almost every cancer there is a website and the American Cancer Society has it all. Yours doctors have or know where to tell you to go for such information. The internet, by the click of button has many. One of the most effective sources is hearing from a friend or family member who has gone through that experience or health fairs. We live in a world where we have various medium to get education and one has the freedom to choose.

Here are some of the popular websites I had visited.

- www.debreastcancer.org - Delaware Breast Cancer Society
- www.wellnessdelaware.org - The wellness Community

THE FACES OF STRUGGLES SUCH AS CANCERS

ARE ON THE JOURNEY TO GOD'S GLORY!

Alfancena Millicent Barrett

- www.lls.org - The Leukemia & Lymphoma Society
- www.cancer.org - American Cancer Society
- www.sistersonamission.org

THE FACES OF STRUGGLES SUCH AS CANCERS

ARE ON THE JOURNEY TO GOD'S GLORY!

Alfancena Millicent Barrett

PICTURES OF MY SCARS

THE FACES OF STRUGGLES SUCH AS CANCERS
ARE ON THE JOURNEY TO GOD'S GLORY!

Alfancena Millicent Barrett

God in His wisdom created us that we can still function without parts of bodies. When the Spirit of God lives within a scar body does not prevent the reflection of the Holy Spirit. The first time one of my aunts saw my scared body, she started praising God. She was praising God for my life and not my body.

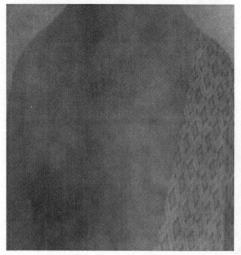

Mastectomy of My Right Breast

THE FACES OF STRUGGLES SUCH AS CANCERS
ARE ON THE JOURNEY TO GOD'S GLORY!

Alfancena Millicent Barrett

Failed Reconstruction and
Hysterectomy

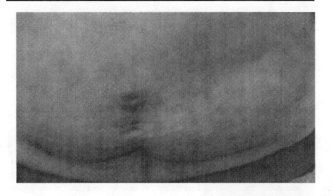

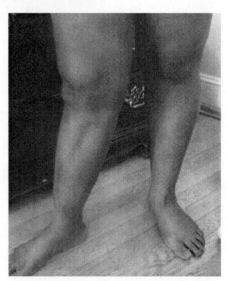

Straightening of My Right Leg

PICTURES OF MY FAMILY

THE FACES OF STRUGGLES SUCH AS CANCERS
ARE ON THE JOURNEY TO GOD'S GLORY!

Alfancena Millicent Barrett

My mom on one of her visit to the United States

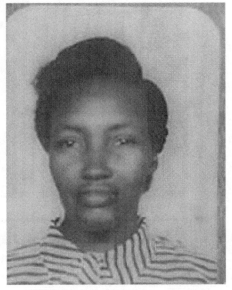

My mom as a young adult

THE FACES OF STRUGGLES SUCH AS CANCERS
ARE ON THE JOURNEY TO GOD'S GLORY!

Alfancena Millicent Barrett

My mom and I on 76 birthday, 2003. She was battling esophagus cancer, she died later that year

THE FACES OF STRUGGLES SUCH AS CANCERS
ARE ON THE JOURNEY TO GOD'S GLORY!

Alfancena Millicent Barrett

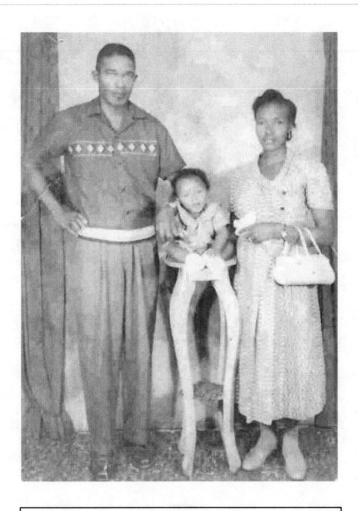

Our most famous family picture, my dad, older brother and mom. It hard to believe that all three are gone.

THE FACES OF STRUGGLES SUCH AS CANCERS
ARE ON THE JOURNEY TO GOD'S GLORY!
Alfancena Millicent Barrett

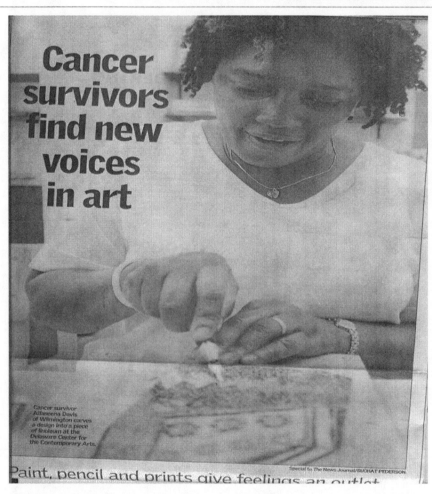

Cancer survivor
Alfancena Davis
of Wilmington carves
a design into a piece
of linoleum at the
Delaware Center for
the Contemporary Arts.

Special to The News Journal/SUCHAT PEDERSON

Paint, pencil and prints give feelings an outlet

Featured in the News Journal, 2005 in the company of twelve beautiful ladies who too are survivor.

THE FACES OF STRUGGLES SUCH AS CANCERS
ARE ON THE JOURNEY TO GOD'S GLORY!

Alfancena Millicent Barrett

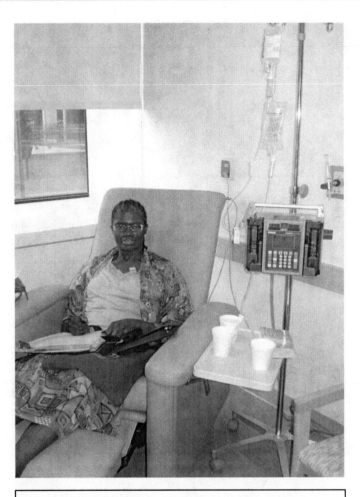

Writing my book while receiving chemo therapy at the University of Pennsylvania

THE FACES OF STRUGGLES SUCH AS CANCERS
ARE ON THE JOURNEY TO GOD'S GLORY!

Alfancena Millicent Barrett

My sister Peaches and I

THE FACES OF STRUGGLES SUCH AS CANCERS
ARE ON THE JOURNEY TO GOD'S GLORY!

Alfancena Millicent Barrett

The last hug I shared with my brother
Villair who is now in glory

THE FACES OF STRUGGLES SUCH AS CANCERS
ARE ON THE JOURNEY TO GOD'S GLORY!

Alfancena Millicent Barrett

My dad with my older
brother's children.

My dad at age eighty-four
standing on the steps my
sister had a good time
chopping on the edges as
little girl.

THE FACES OF STRUGGLES SUCH AS CANCERS
ARE ON THE JOURNEY TO GOD'S GLORY!

Alfancena Millicent Barrett

Nieces and nephews a representation of all my siblings children

Surrounded by my remaining siblings, my dad, nieces, nephews.

THE FACES OF STRUGGLES SUCH AS CANCERS
ARE ON THE JOURNEY TO GOD'S GLORY!

Alfancena Millicent Barrett

My nephew and I who is now my adopted son.

THE FACES OF STRUGGLES SUCH AS CANCERS
ARE ON THE JOURNEY TO GOD'S GLORY!

Alfancena Millicent Barrett

My brother Cleve preparing a meal for me on his first visit to the United States.

THE FACES OF STRUGGLES SUCH AS CANCERS
ARE ON THE JOURNEY TO GOD'S GLORY!

Alfancena Millicent Barrett

My brother Lambert and I visiting our childhood home in 2006

THE FACES OF STRUGGLES SUCH AS CANCERS ARE ON THE JOURNEY TO GOD'S GLORY!

Alfancena Millicent Barrett

My nieces and nephews

Me with my younger brother and my niece.

THE FACES OF STRUGGLES SUCH AS CANCERS
ARE ON THE JOURNEY TO GOD'S GLORY!
Alfancena Millicent Barrett

Me at fourteen years old with my cousins

ABOUT THE AUTHOR

Each time I told my story I was encouraged to write a book. I questioned myself how could I write a book? I did not like writing and often times my English was not so great. So I never seriously thought about it. When I was attacked with Lymphoma cancer for the third time and the fifth time to fight cancer I started praying about the prospect of really telling my story in written form. The title of the book I received in a dream and almost everything else came to me when I woke up in the morning's fresh on my mind as if I spent time thinking about it during my last treatment. I truly believe I was spiritually directed.

How could I not share my story after being a survivor of three cancers and one who has faced medical adversities since my childhood. I decided to tell my testimony in written form. It tells how my faith in God made a difference in my life. First girl and third child of Roslyn and Victor Barrett. Graduate of Mount Nebo Primary, Guy's Hill High, Saint Joseph Teachers' College (Jamaica) and Delaware Technical and Community

THE FACES OF STRUGGLES SUCH AS CANCERS
ARE ON THE JOURNEY TO GOD'S GLORY!

Alfancena Millicent Barrett

College. I achieved my Associates Degrees in Early Childhood Education (SUMMA CUM LAUDE) and Human Services (MAGNA CUM LAUDE) I made the Dean's list each semester while in college and the Governor's list twice. I am an accomplished, creative, and dedicated Early Childhood (infant) teacher. Most of all I am a servant in the role of a Deaconess in God's Kingdom at Shiloh Baptist Church, Wilmington, Delaware.

My hope is, by sharing my story will give others the understanding that there is no valley that can be too deep, no mountains too high, and no path too difficult that God will not see you through. Especially when I am aware that the closer I walked with God the test will never be over until He calls me home.

LaVergne, TN USA
26 July 2010
190903LV00004B/4/P